Idioches

Diagrapharted

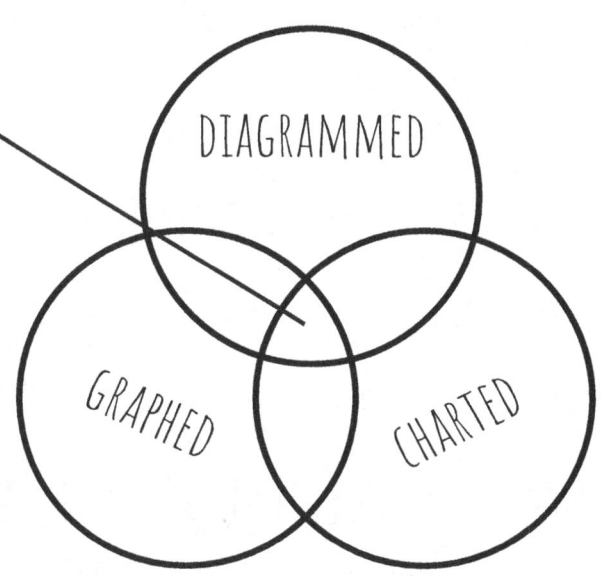

By: Matt Weber

ISBN: 978-1-949356-02-1

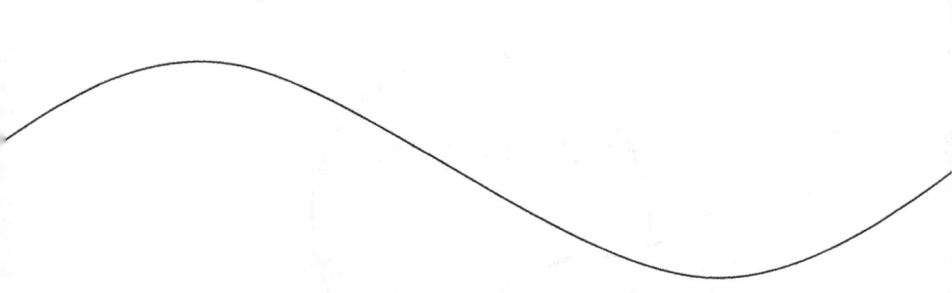

This book is dedicated to Jeff Han

THE GUY WHO WAS BORN AT THE RIGHT TIME

FOREWORD

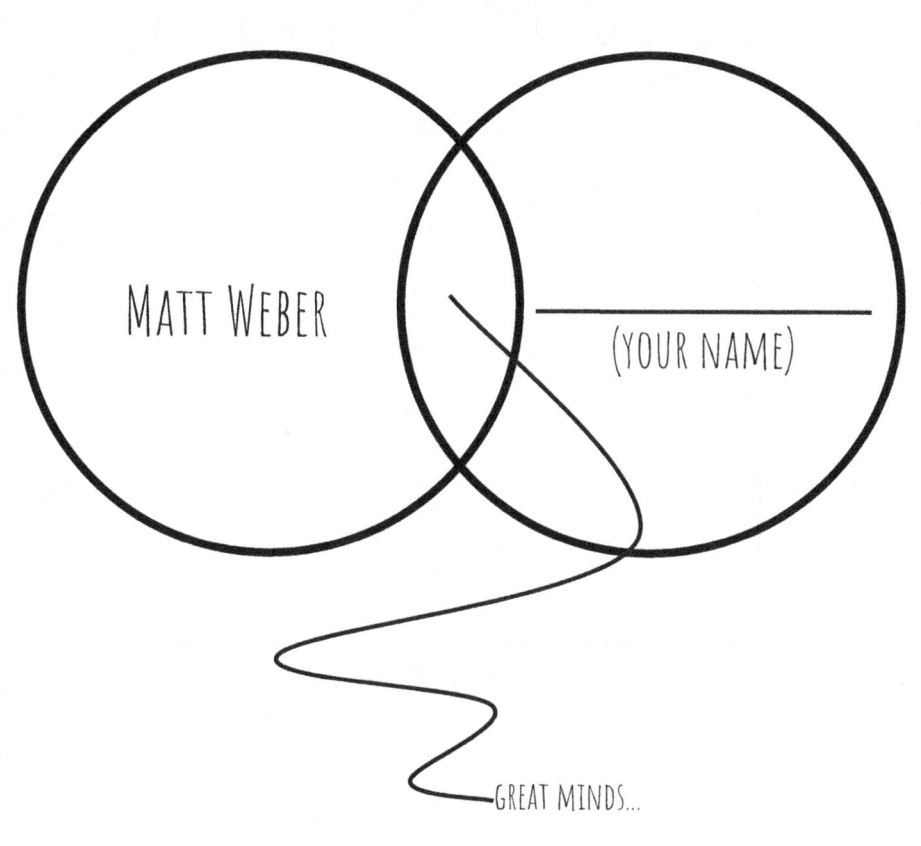

EUPHEMISMS FOR "NOT A CHANCE!"

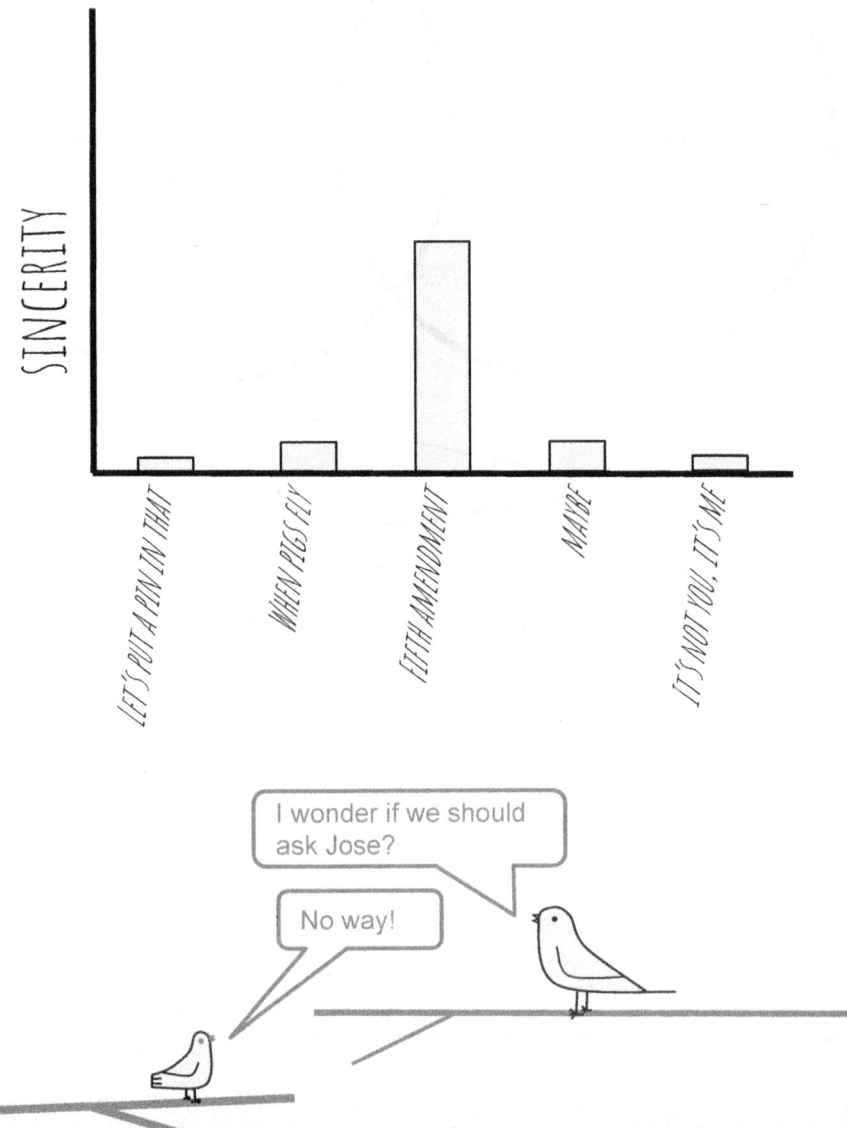

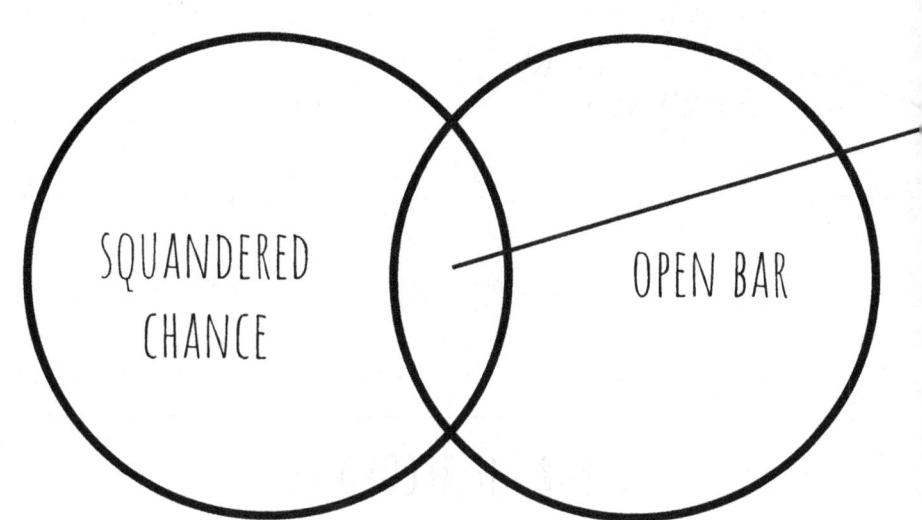

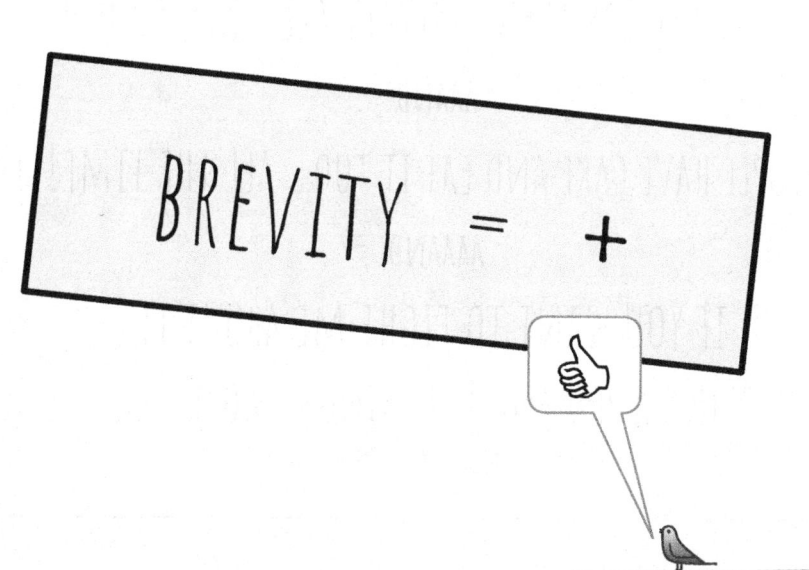

WASTED
OPPORTUNITY

FOR THE RECORD...

I'VE NEVER SEEN A CLOUD WITH A SILVER LINING,
LET ALONE EVERY CLOUD!

AAND...

CUCUMBERS AREN'T REALLY ALL *THAT* COOL!!

AAAND...

PEOPLE HAVE CAKE AND EAT IT TOO... ALL THE TIME!!!

AAAAND...

IF YOU WANT TO FIGHT ME ABOUT IT...

YOU BRING A PEN AND I'LL BRING A SWORD...(PIECE OF CAKE)

(AND AS LONG AS IT'S NOT A GUNFIGHT)

Cutting

THE CHEESE

	DO	DON'T
CAN		
CAN'T	YOU REALLY STINK!	

THE MUSTARD

Woof!

CLOTHES MAKE THE MAN

CAN'T JUDGE A BOOK BY ITS COVER

If you're reading this, you must have made some judgment about the word "Diagrapharted" on the cover.

Yup!

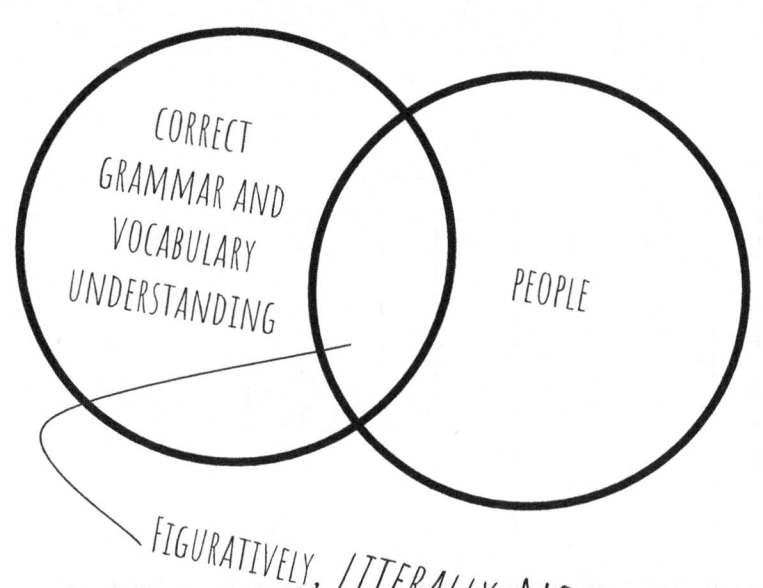

CORRECT GRAMMAR AND VOCABULARY UNDERSTANDING

PEOPLE

FIGURATIVELY, LITERALLY, NOBODY

ROWHENME

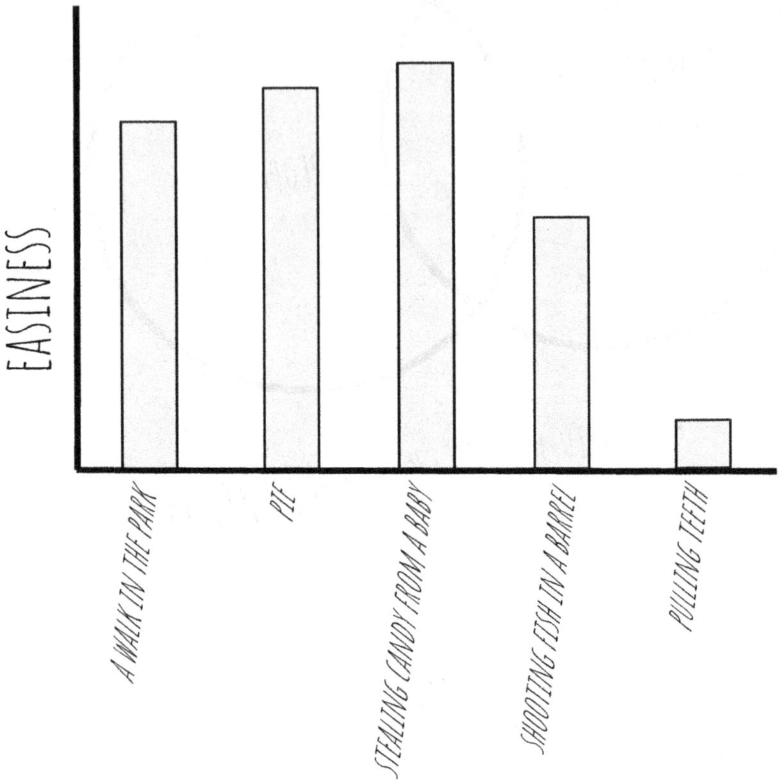

EASINESS

A WALK IN THE PARK

PIE

STEALING CANDY FROM A BABY

SHOOTING FISH IN A BARREL

PULLING TEETH

PRIDE...FALL

BLACK

Dogs

	YOUNG	OLD
NEW	✔	✘
OLD	✔	✔

TRICKS

NUMBER 1

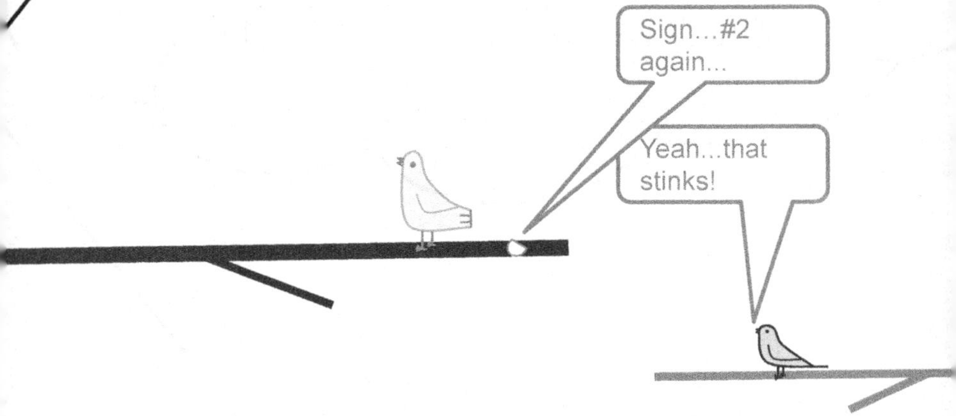

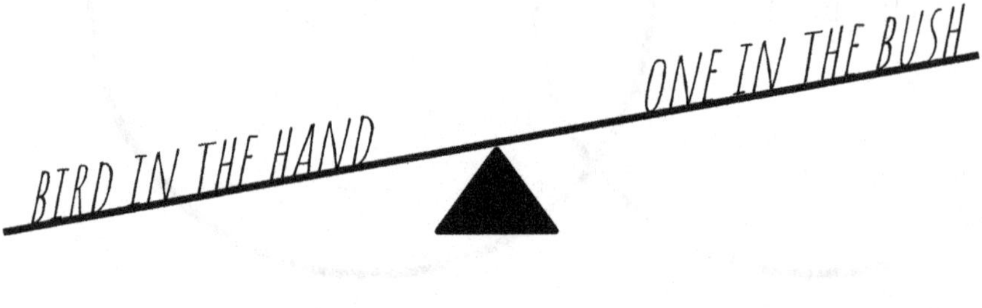

Up-Mixed Idioms

I'm no rocket surgeon!

Don't spill the cat out of the bag of beans!

Don't count your chicken eggs in one basket!

I wasn't born falling off a turnip truck yesterday!

It was so quiet I could hear a mouse drop.

Beat a dead horse with the ugly stick

HIT

PRODUCTIVENESS

- The nail on the head
- The road

- The hay
- Below the belt

PAIN

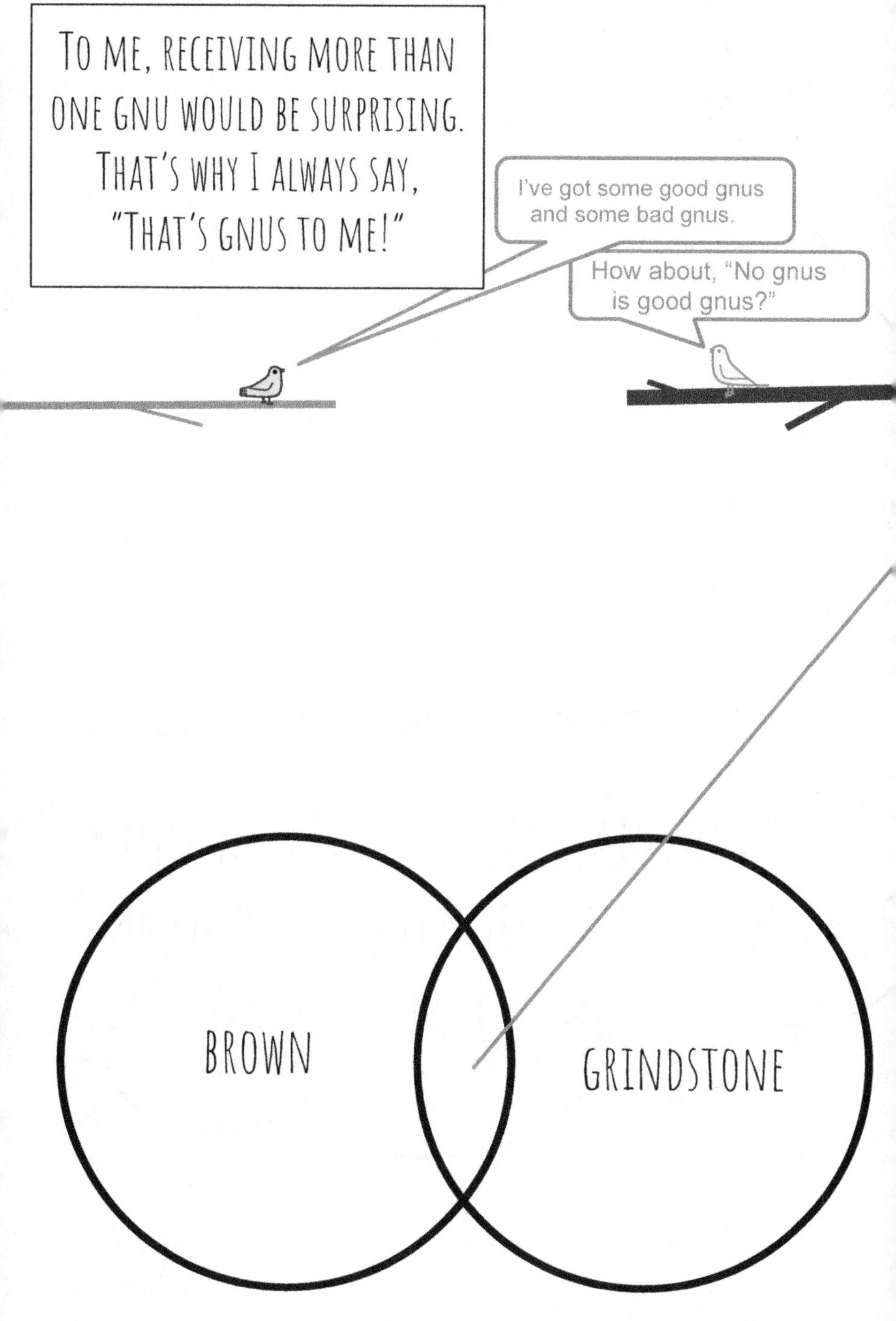
TO ME, RECEIVING MORE THAN ONE GNU WOULD BE SURPRISING. THAT'S WHY I ALWAYS SAY, "THAT'S GNUS TO ME!"
I've got some good gnus and some bad gnus.
How about, "No gnus is good gnus?"
BROWN
GRINDSTONE

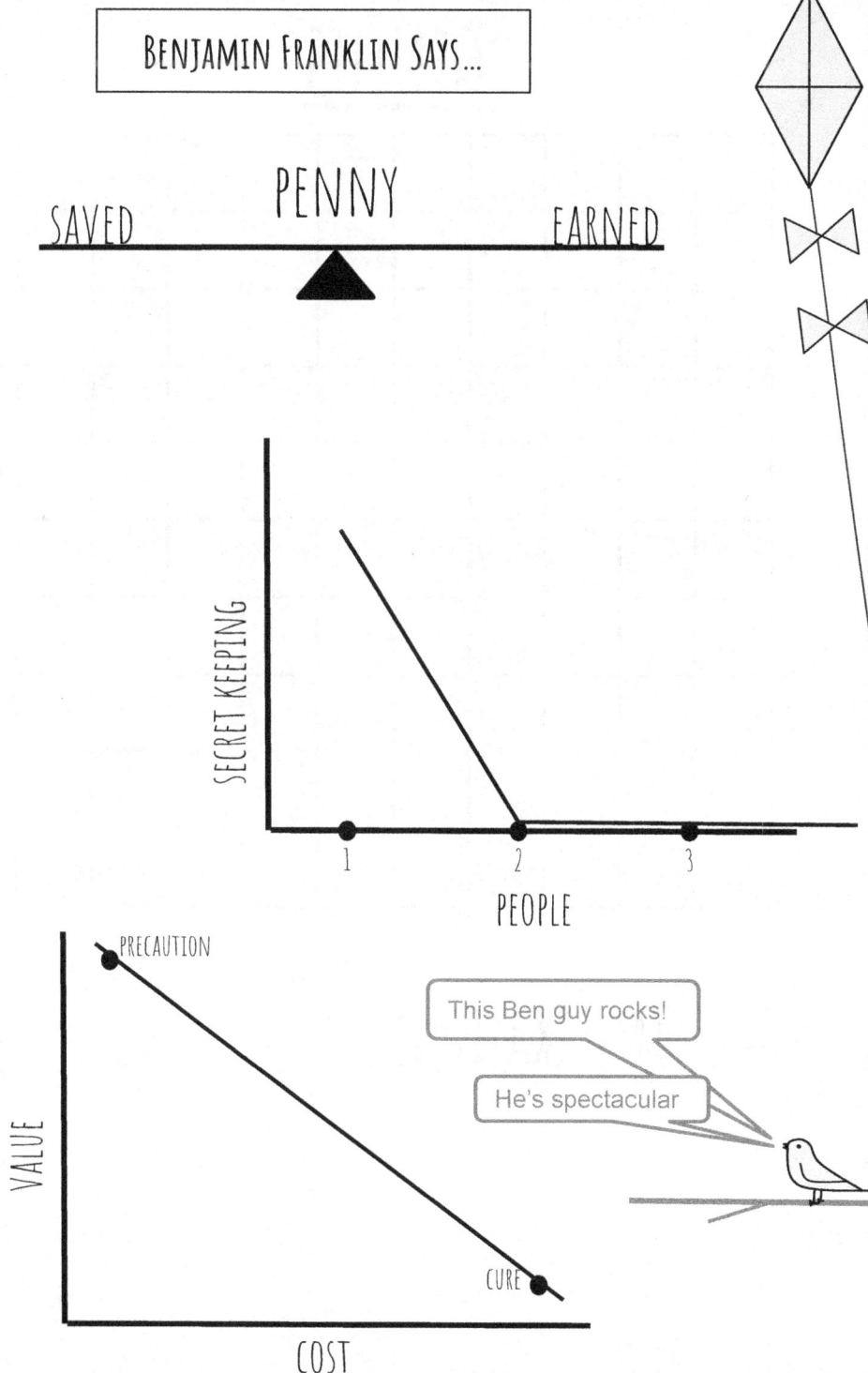

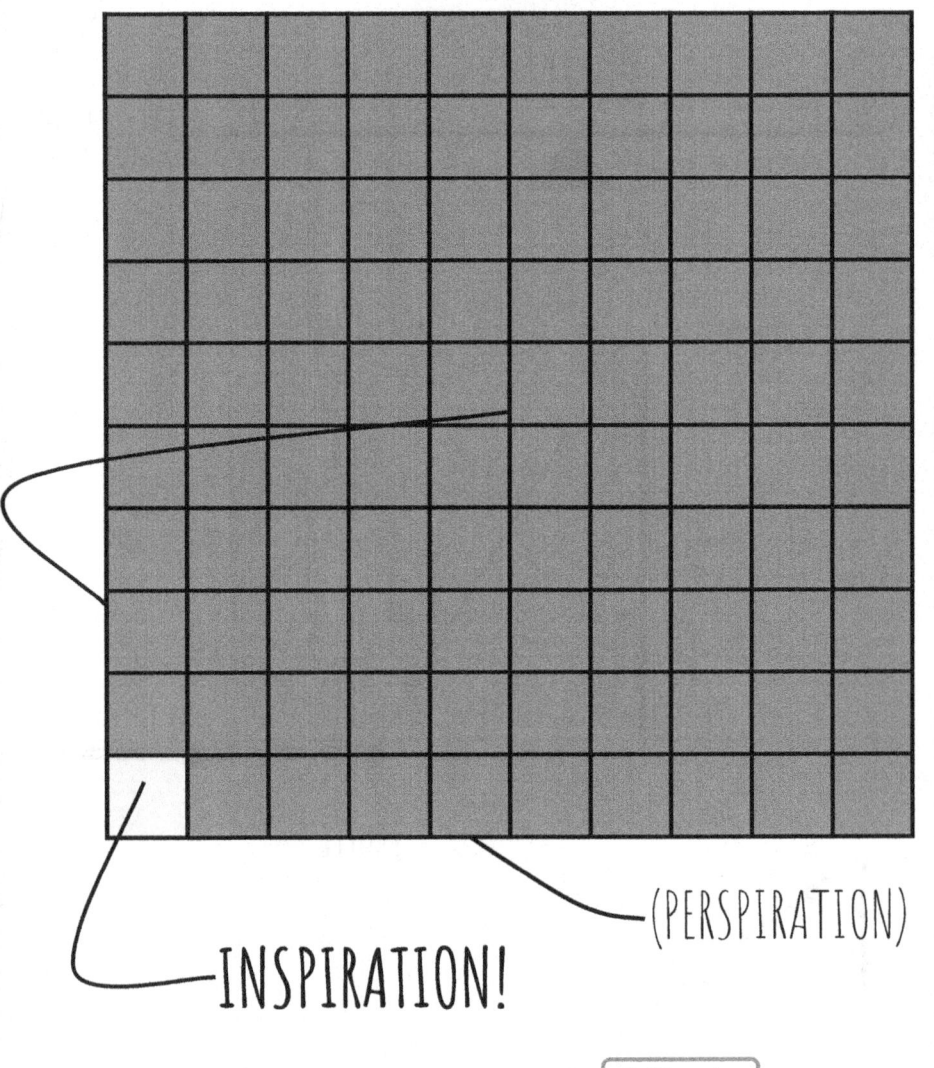

ONE TIME I GOT OUT OF DEBT UNEXPECTEDLY; IT WAS OUT OF THE PURPLE. (OUT OF THE RED OUT OF THE BLUE)

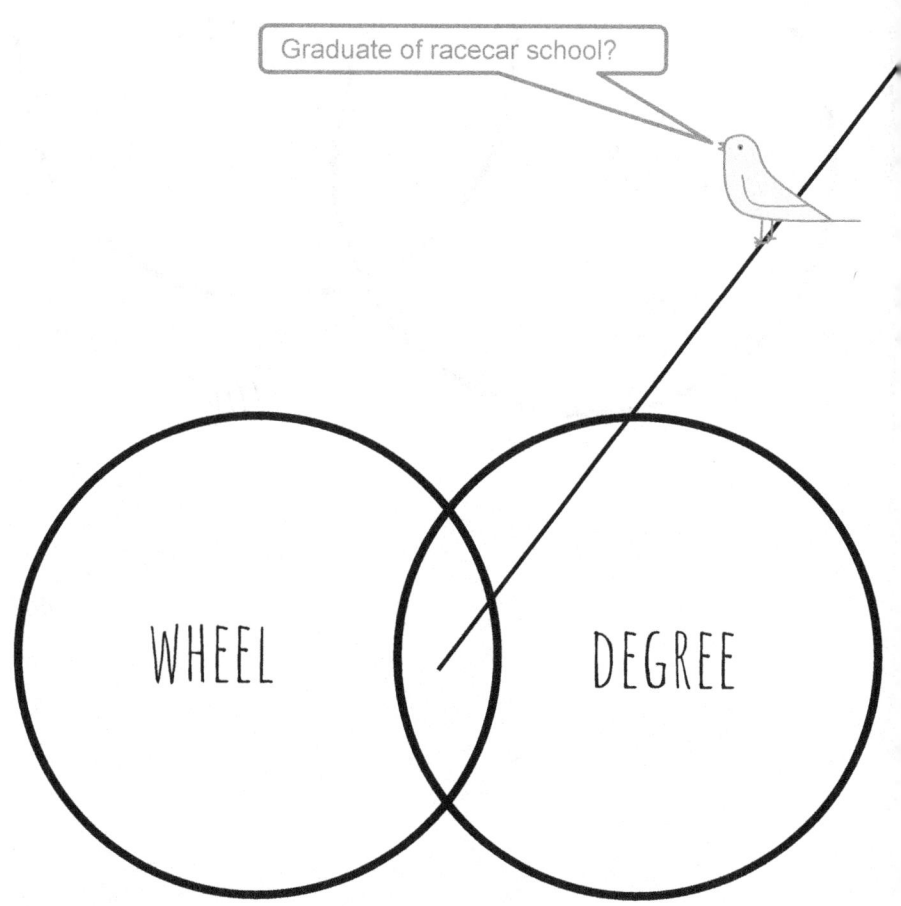

THIRD

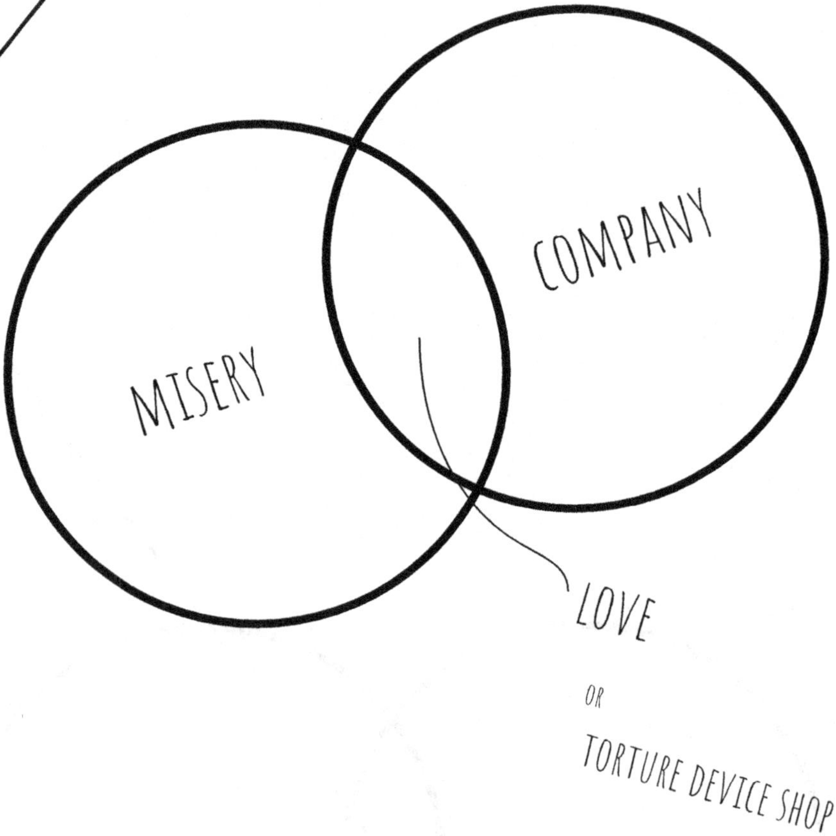

COMPANY

MISERY

LOVE

OR

TORTURE DEVICE SHOP

Random axe of kindness?

I TRIED... TO INTEGRATE GENDER EQUALITY INTO IDIOMS.
BUT IT DIDN'T REALLY WORK OUT.
I USED TO SAY, "HE'S GREAT! HE'D GIVE YOU THE SHIRT OFF HIS BACK."
I SWITCHED IT TO, "SHE'S GREAT! SHE'D GIVE YOU THE SHIRT OFF HER BACK."
FOR SOME REASON, PEOPLE DIDN'T SEEM TO APPRECIATE MY NEUTRALITY.

If you teach a woman to fish...

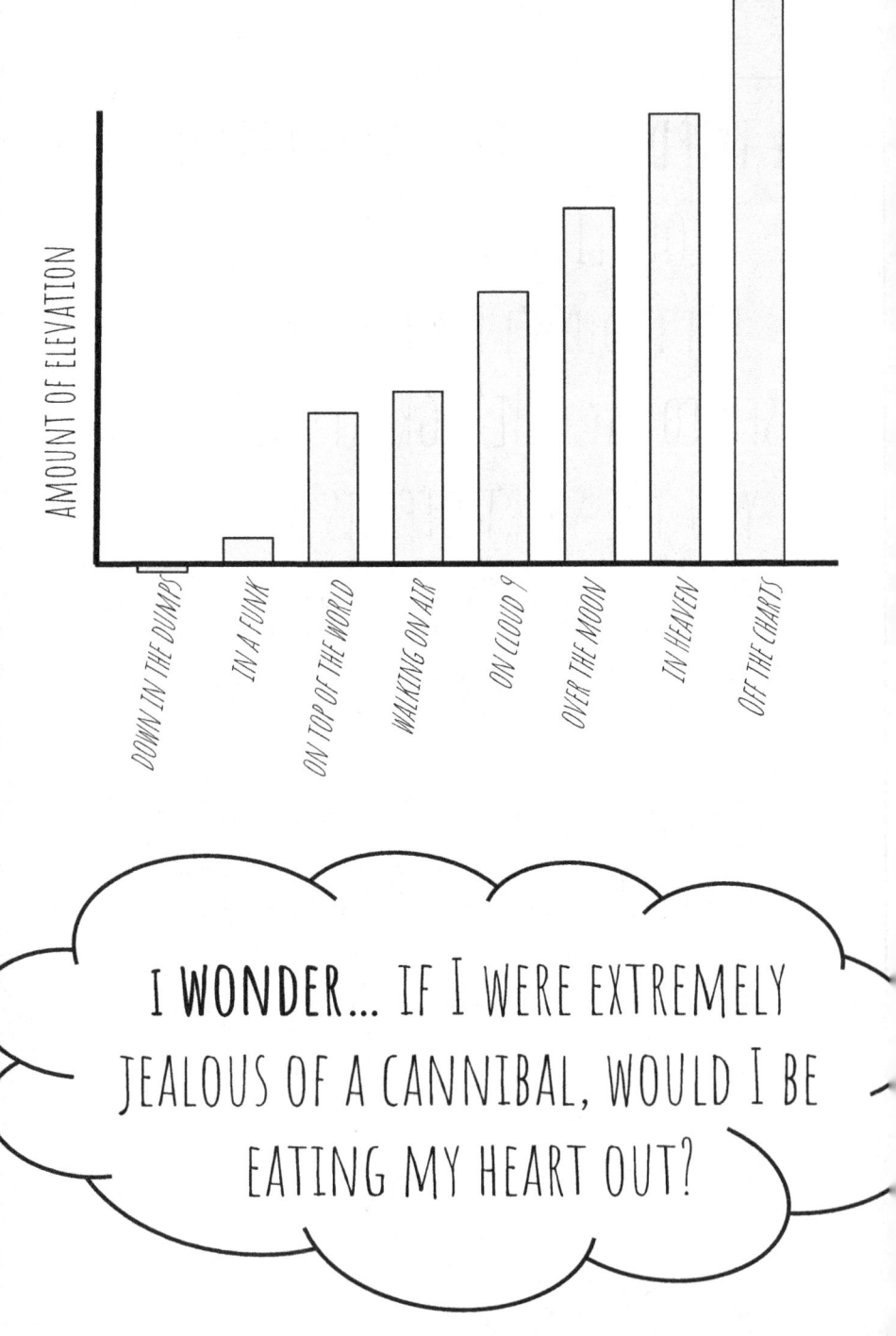

A L L

T H I N G S

"OUR RELATIONSHIP IS GOING QUITE POORLY."

"I WOULD PREFER MY DRINK TO BE COLD AND SLIGHTLY WATERED DOWN."

IF I WERE A LION, I'D NEVER WANT TO ADMIT THAT I WAS WRONG...

IF IT MEANT THAT I HAD TO SWALLOW MY PRIDE!

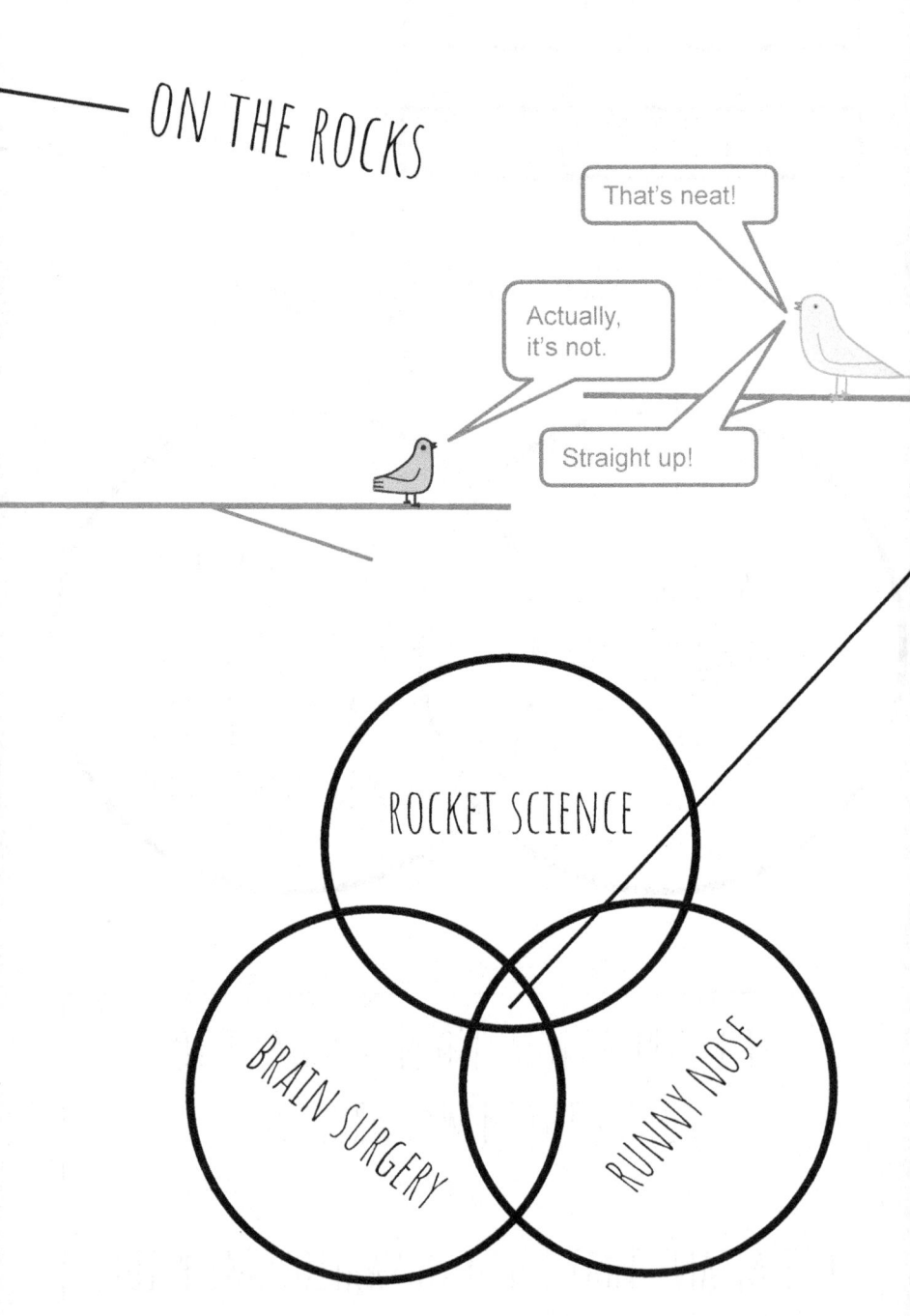

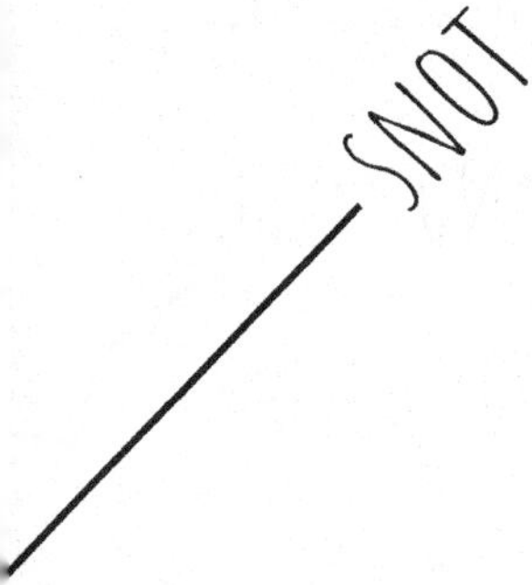
SNOT

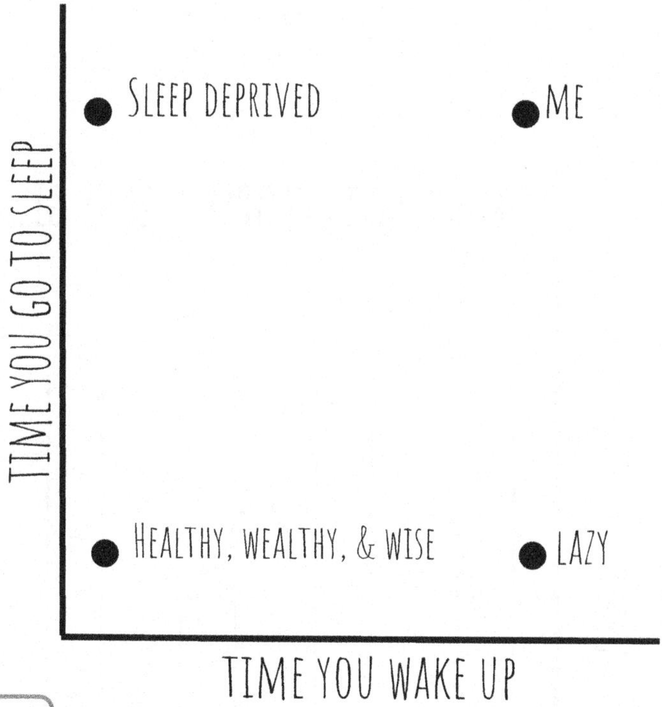
SLEEP DEPRIVED
ME
HEALTHY, WEALTHY, & WISE
LAZY
TIME YOU GO TO SLEEP
TIME YOU WAKE UP

I got up early!

IF THE PEN IS MIGHTIER THAN THE SWORD, AND A PICTURE IS WORTH A THOUSAND WORDS, IS A PICTURE OF A PEN WORTH 1000 SWORDS?

BODY PARTS PEOPLE MIGHT GIVE YOU

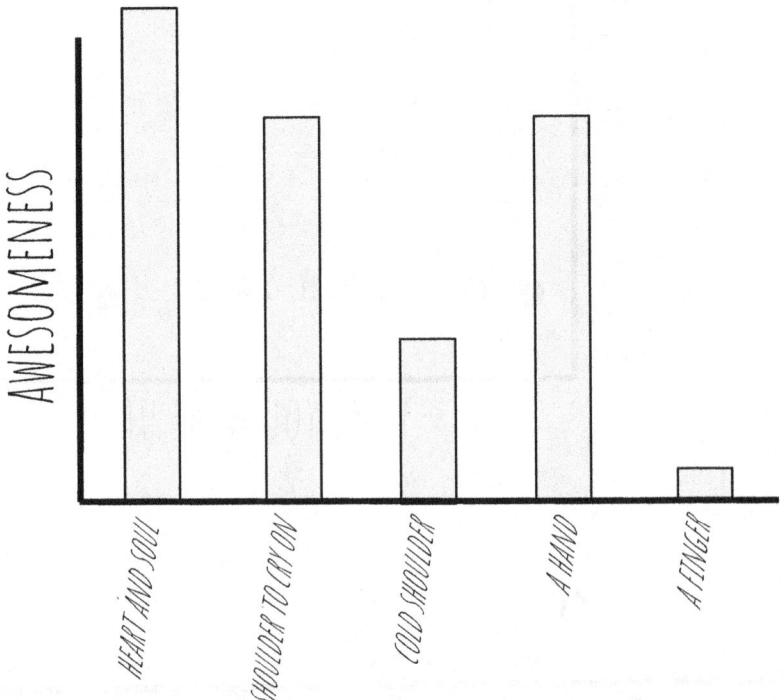

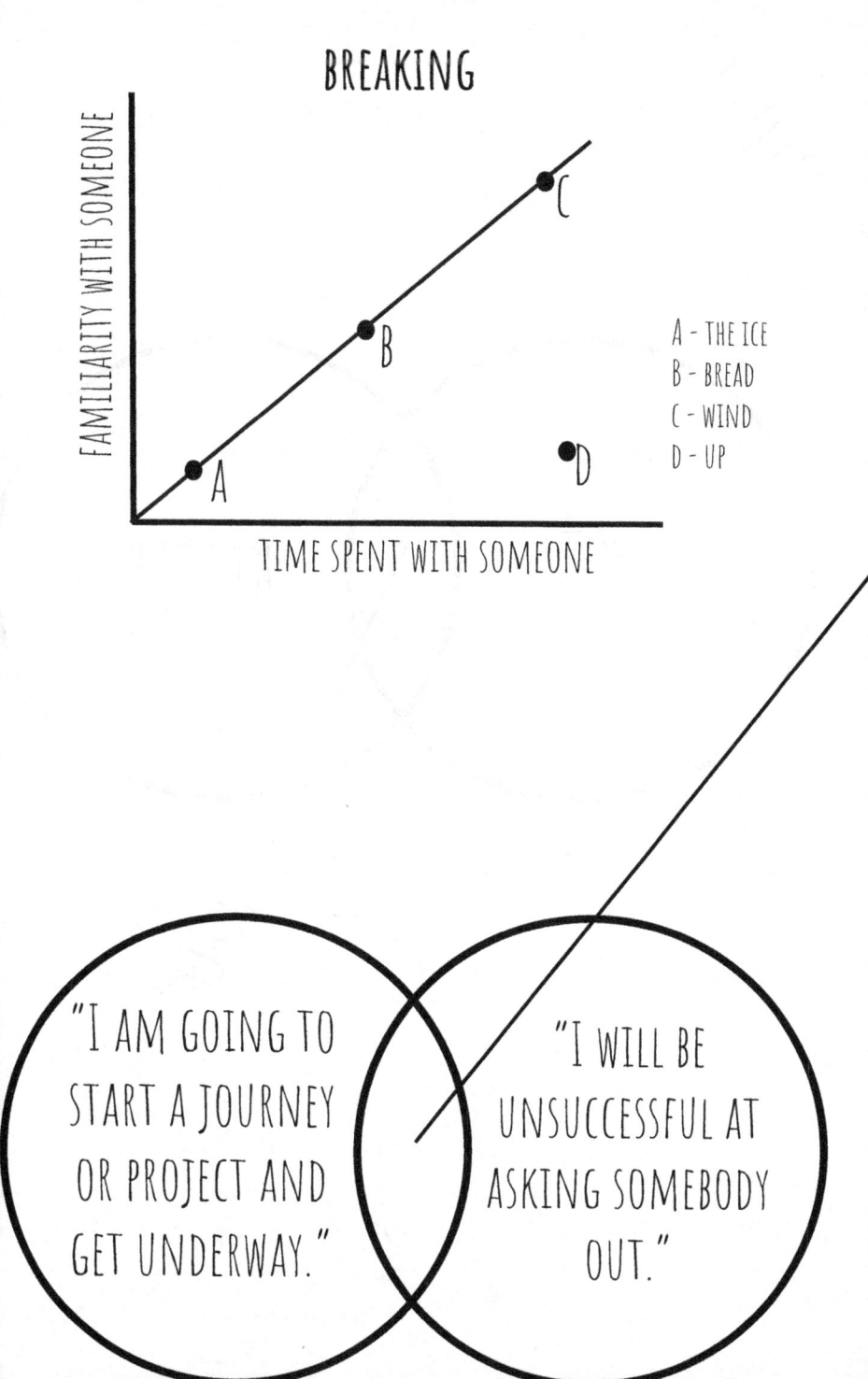

— STRIKE OUT

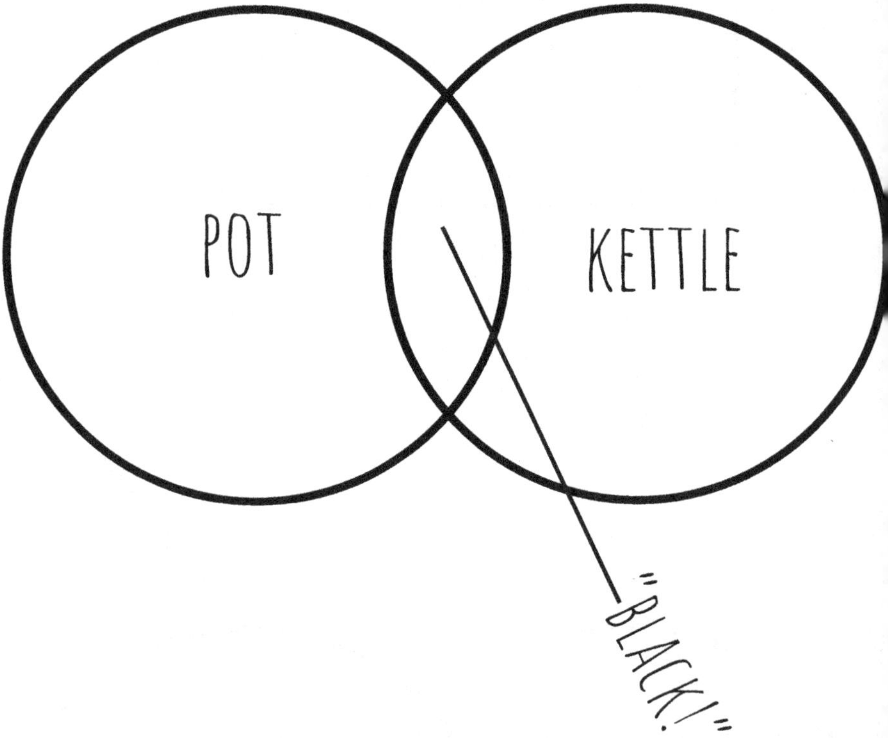

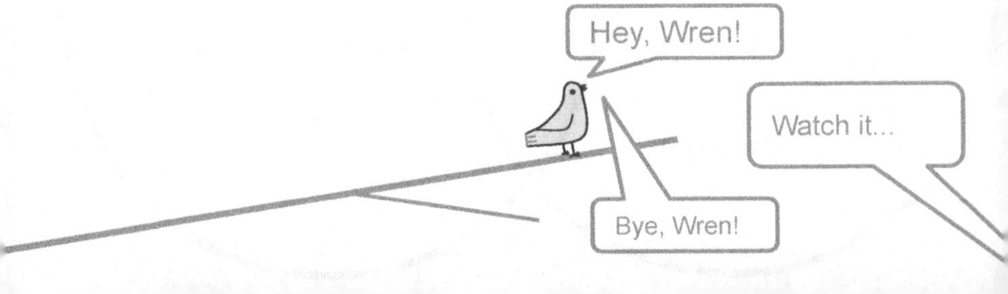

I **WONDER**... WHAT DO BIRDS CALL ANOTHER BIRD THAT KISSES UP TO THE BOSS OR TEACHER?

A *WHITE-NOSER?*

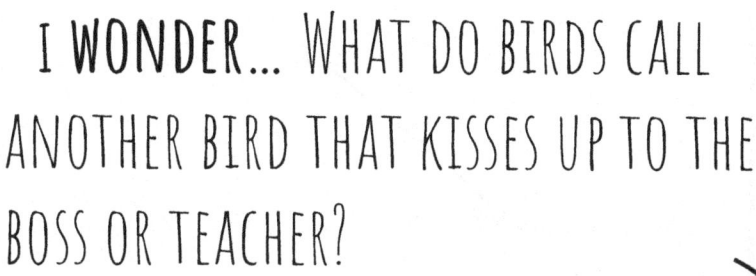

I wonder what donkeys call that?

YOU KNOW WHAT I ALWAYS SAY...

IN THE LAND OF THE BLIND,

ONLY THE KING IS THE TARGET AUDIENCE FOR THIS BOOK!

Market research was never really my strong suit.

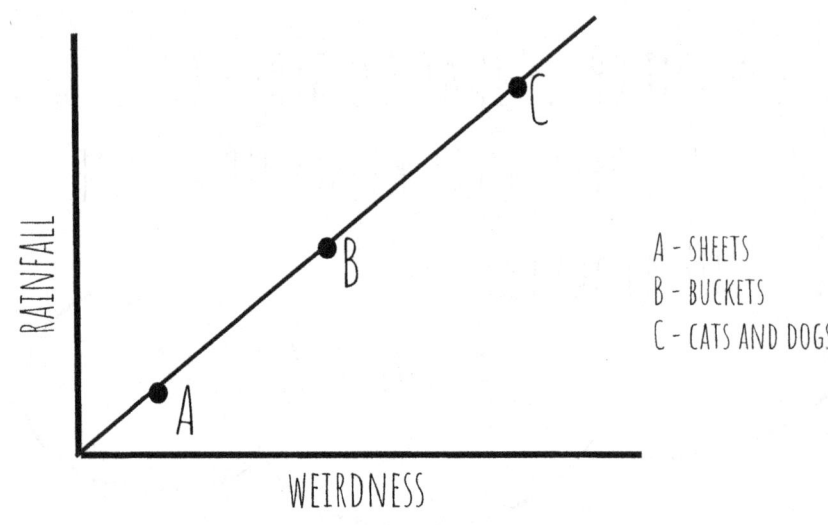

RAINFALL

WEIRDNESS

A - SHEETS
B - BUCKETS
C - CATS AND DOGS

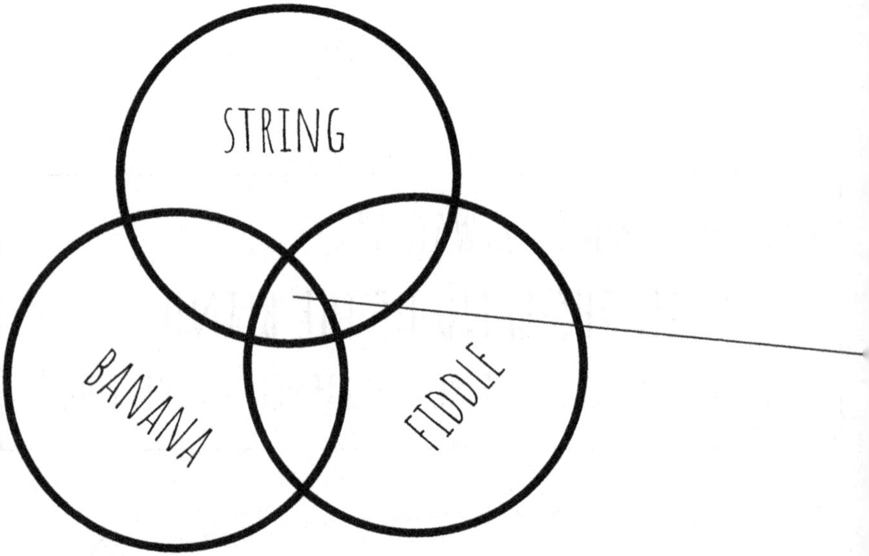

STRING

BANANA

FIDDLE

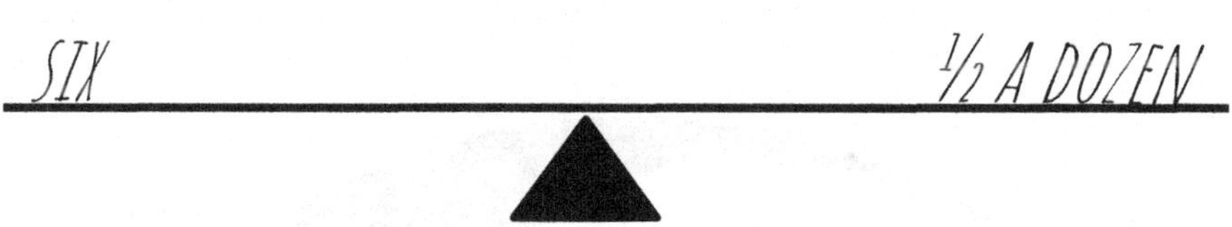

HAND GRENADES

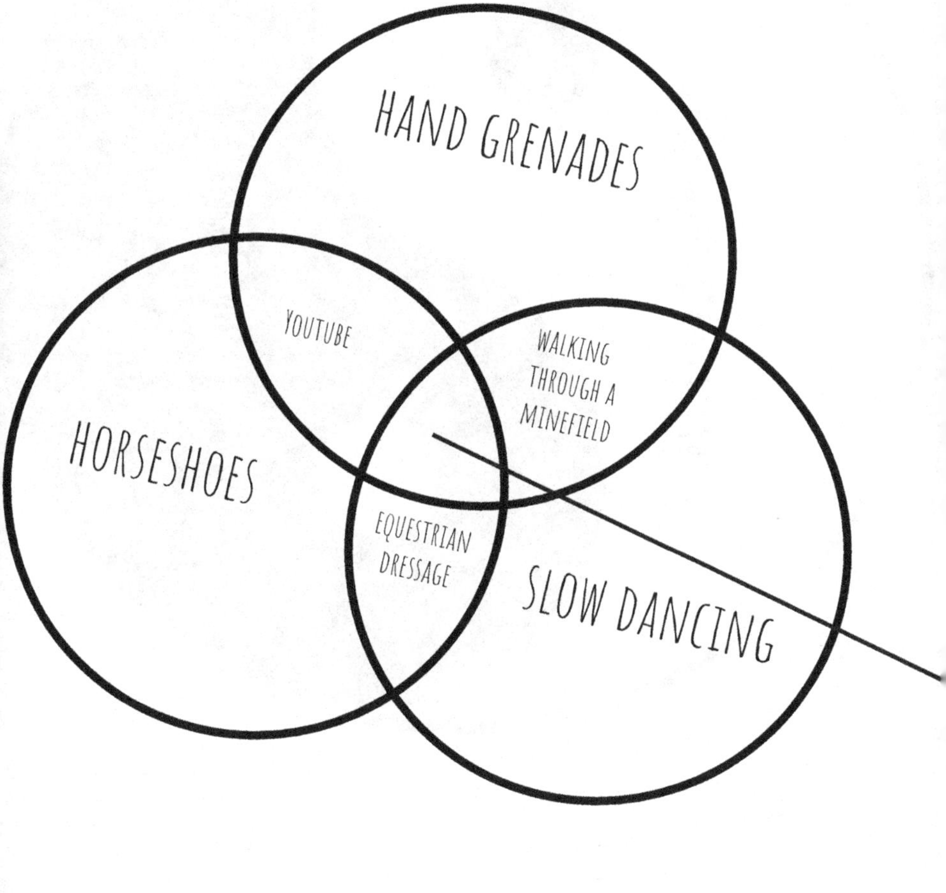

YOUTUBE

WALKING
THROUGH A
MINEFIELD

HORSESHOES

EQUESTRIAN
DRESSAGE

SLOW DANCING

—2ND

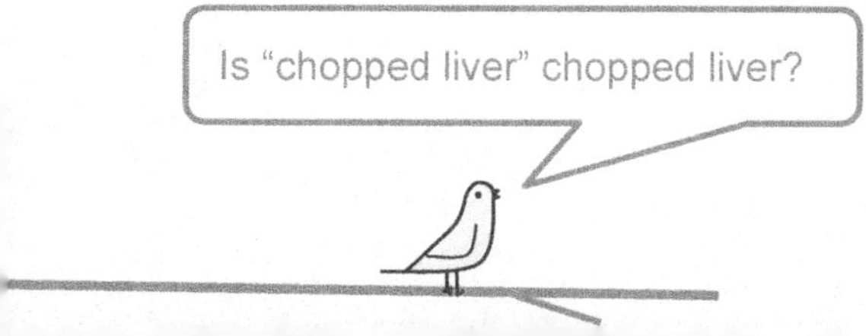

Is "chopped liver" chopped liver?

NOTHING VENTURED NOTHING GAINED
BETTER SAFE THAN SORRY
CLOSE
No cigar!?

In ancient China, when women had bound feet, and a woman had to take the place of another woman who was held in high regard, would they say, "She has small shoes to fill!"?

If somebody were to take the place of an esteemed pirate who had a peg leg, would they say, "He has a big shoe to fill!"?

I feel sorry for the sasquatch who's next in line!

YOUR ANTS PANTS

I WAS THINKING... WHEN SOMEBODY'S USING THE WORD
"LITERALLY"
WAY TOO MUCH,

THEY ARE A LITTLE LITERALLY LITERARILY ILLITERATE.

The way I figure it, that is some lateral thinking. Or, "out of the box" figuratively. Because, it was literally inside the box.

IF... SOMEBODY IS REALLY GOOD AT GARDENING BUT ALSO REALLY CLUMSY, ARE THEY ALL GREEN THUMBS?

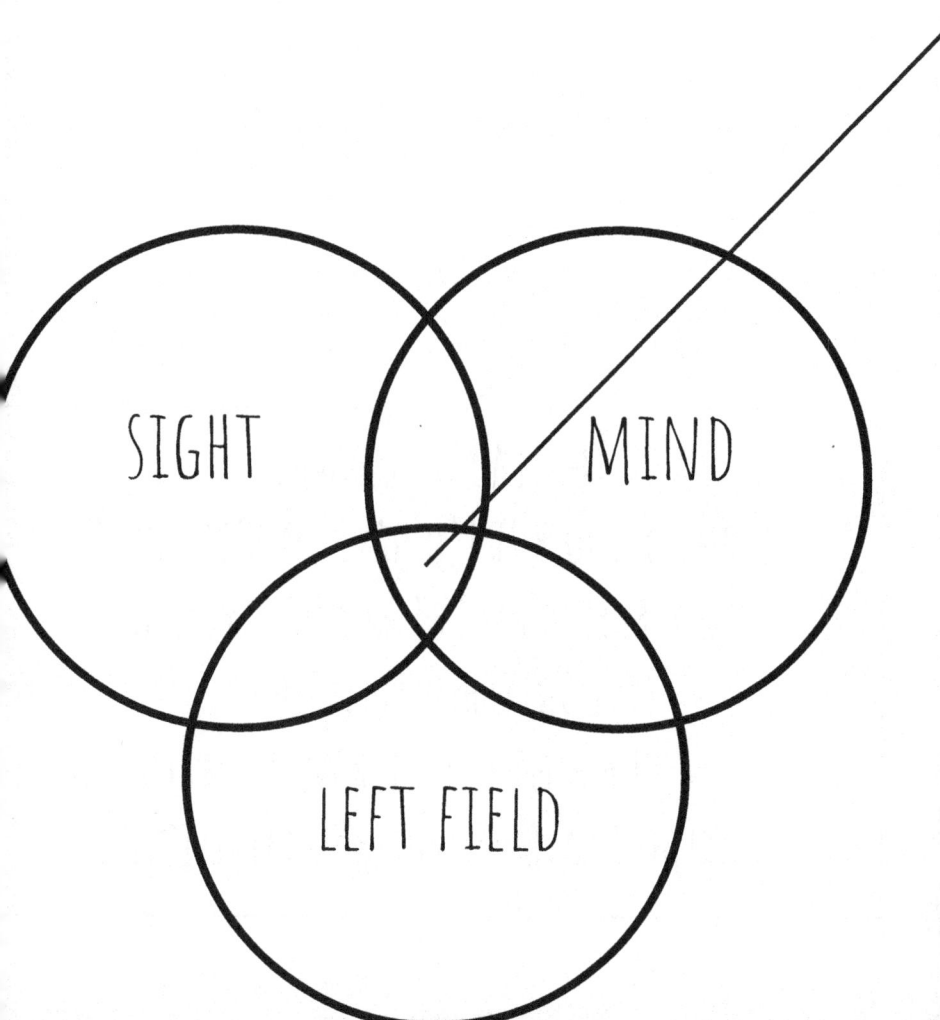

That amazingly seemingly came from nowhere!

INSTEAD OF SAYING,
"I'D TELL YOU BUT I'D HAVE TO KILL YOU,"
WHICH EVERYBODY IS TIRED OF HEARING,
I'VE SWITCHED TO SAYING,
"I'D GIVE YOU A HINT BUT I'D HAVE TO MAIM YOU."
IT REALLY CATCHES PEOPLE'S ATTENTION.

	BIRDS	WORMS
a.m.	SUCCEED	DIE
p.m.	STARVE	SUCCEED

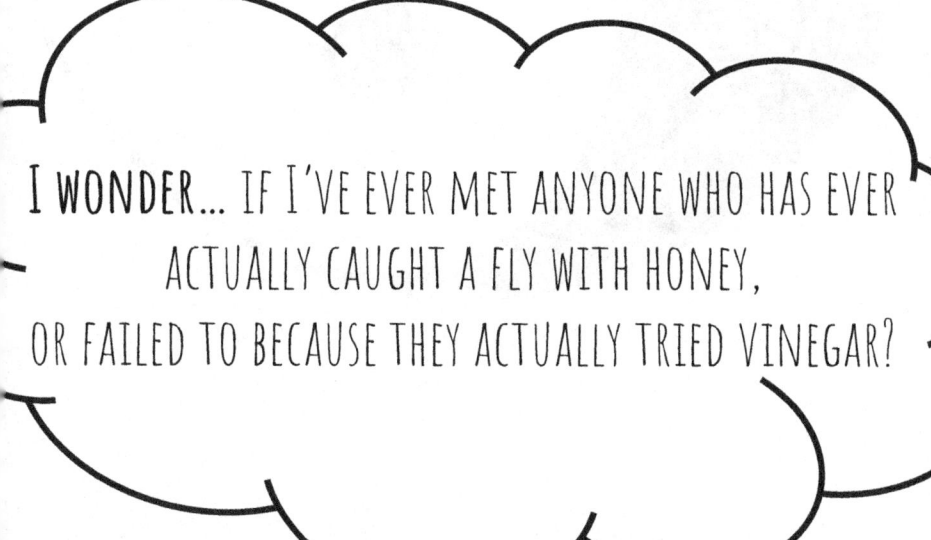

I WONDER... IF I'VE EVER MET ANYONE WHO HAS EVER ACTUALLY CAUGHT A FLY WITH HONEY, OR FAILED TO BECAUSE THEY ACTUALLY TRIED VINEGAR?

ABSENCE MAKES THE HEART GROW FONDER

OUT OF SIGHT OUT OF MIND

BOOKS

HAY

ROAD

HIT THE

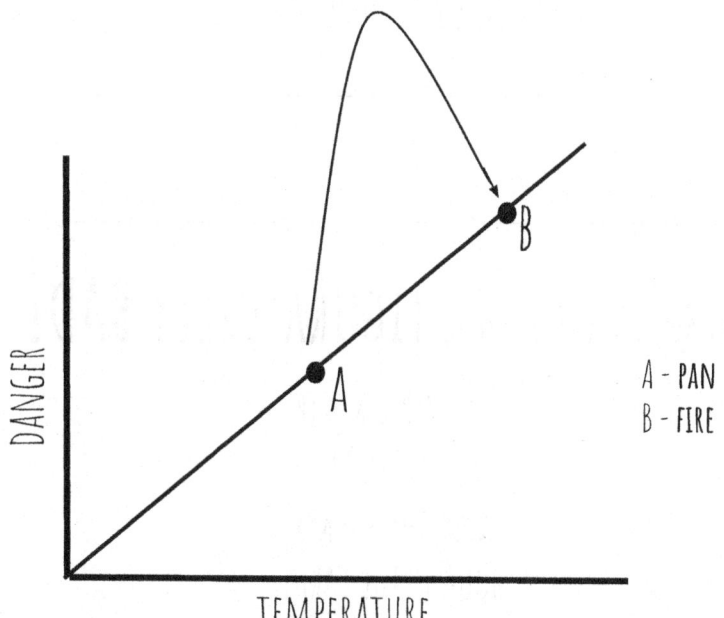

DANGER

TEMPERATURE

A

B

A - PAN
B - FIRE

FIGURATIVELY NOT BAD, LITERALLY BAD!

GOLDEN PARACHUTE
GO OUT ON A LIMB
ON PINS AND NEEDLES
TWO LEFT FEET
THROWING THE BABY OUT WITH THE BATH WATER
PUT YOUR NOSE TO THE GRINDSTONE
CAT GOT YOUR TONGUE
WRAP MY HEAD AROUND IT
WEAR YOUR HEART ON YOUR SLEEVE
BEAT A DEAD HORSE

LITERALLY NOT BAD, FIGURATIVELY BAD!

GOT A PINK SLIP
CHAPTER 11
KICK THE BUCKET
BOUGHT THE FARM

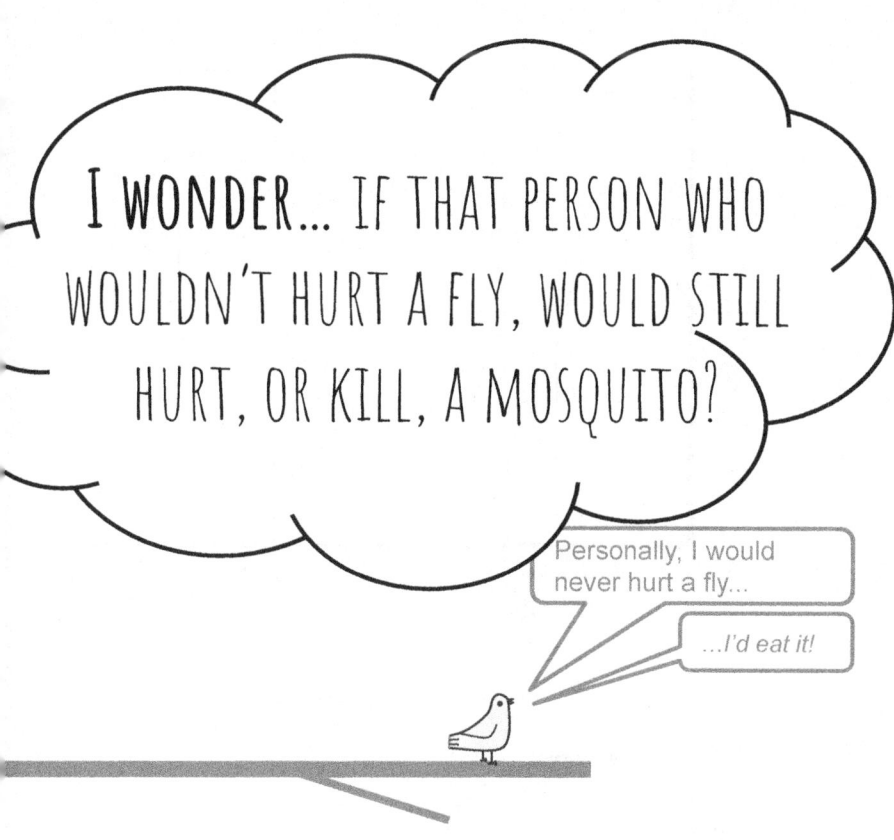

IF I HAD A NICKEL FOR EVERY TIME I... *WONDERED HOW MUCH A NICKEL WOULD BE WORTH IN TODAY'S DOLLARS BACK WHEN THAT IDIOM/CLICHE WAS FIRST STARTED...***I'D HAVE...**ABOUT 35 CENTS.

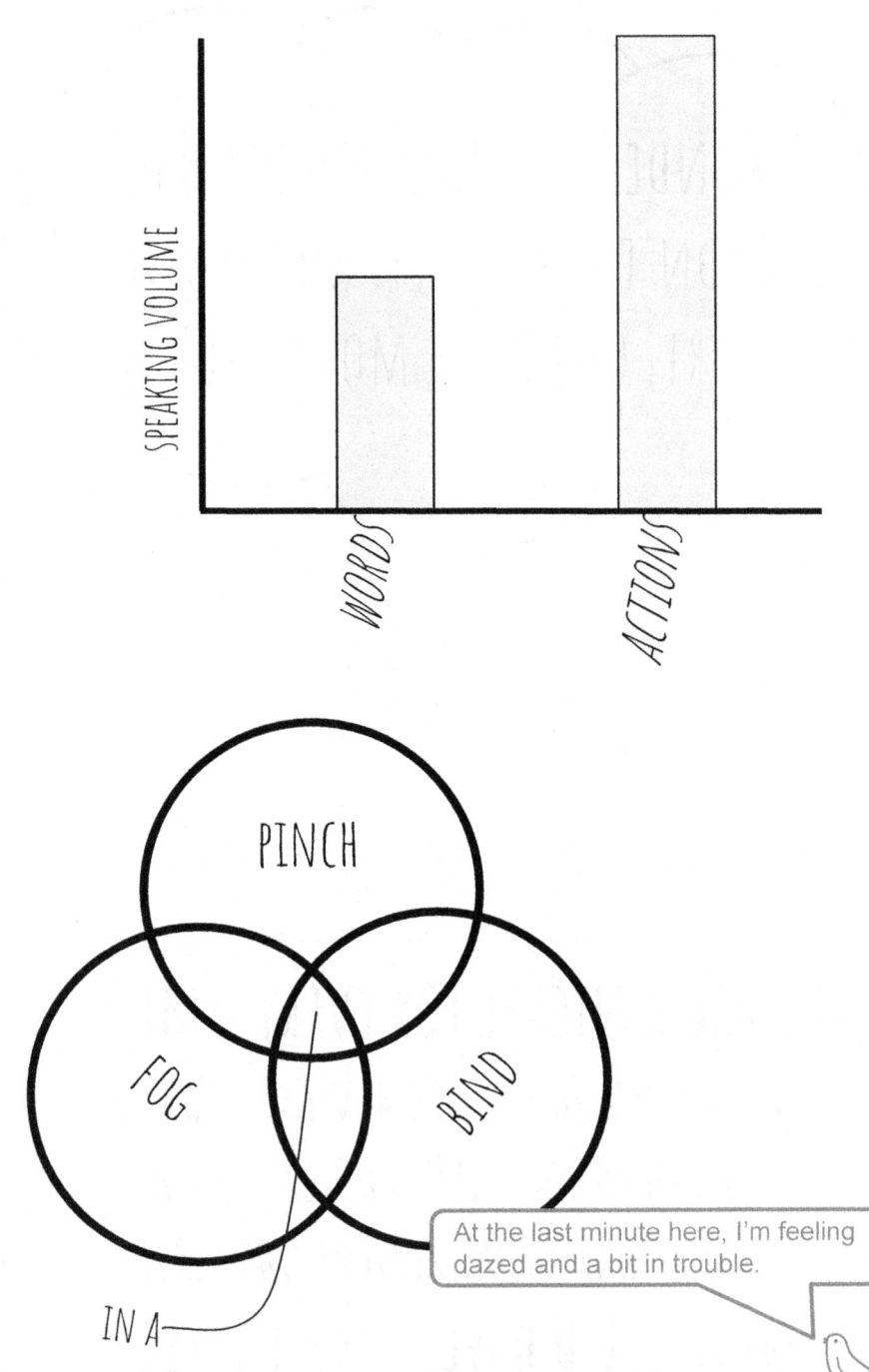

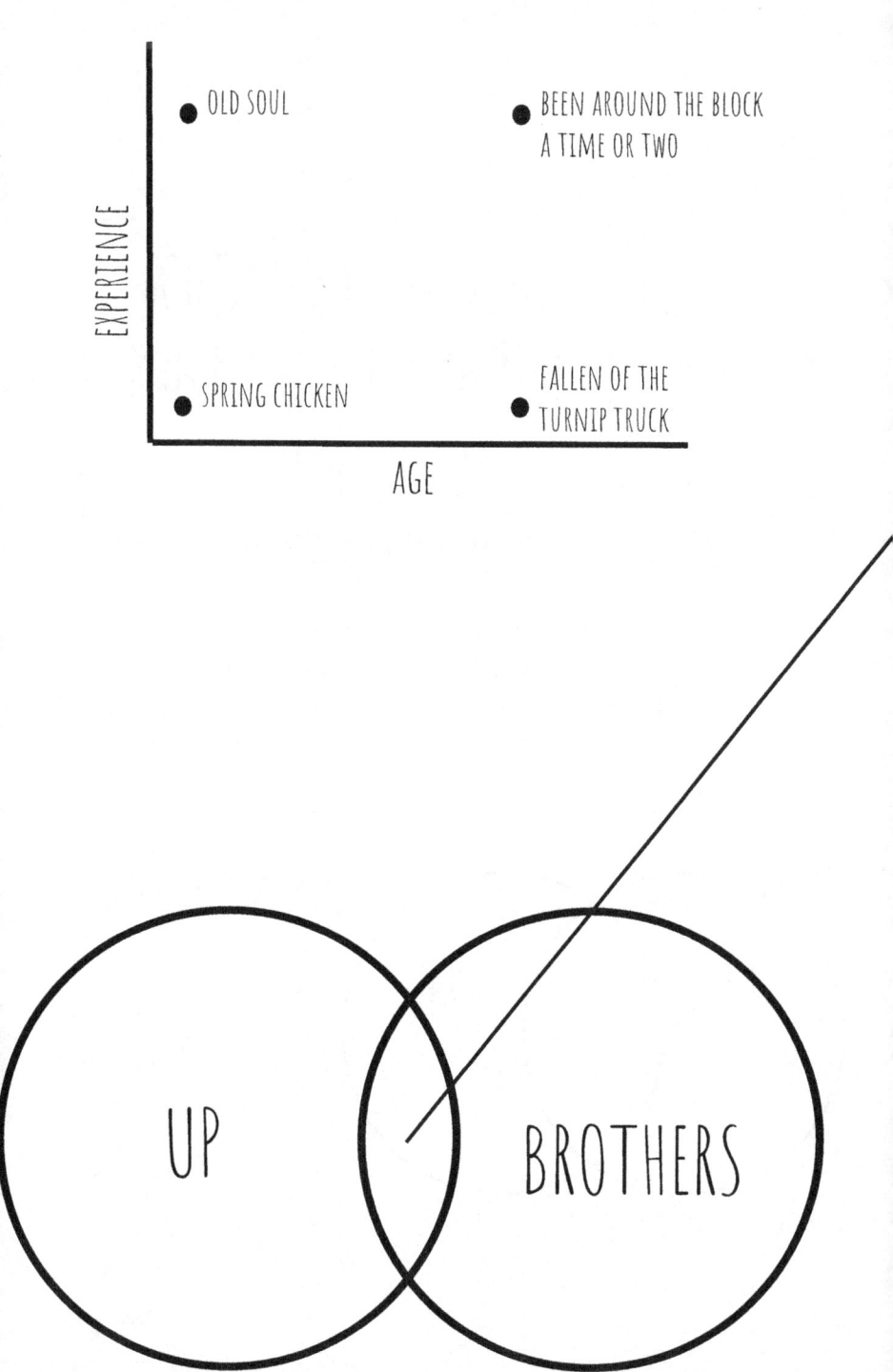

EXPERIENCE

- OLD SOUL
- BEEN AROUND THE BLOCK A TIME OR TWO
- SPRING CHICKEN
- FALLEN OF THE TURNIP TRUCK

AGE

UP

BROTHERS

IN ARMS

PEOPLE WHO **GIVE 110%** DON'T ALWAYS GIVE 110%. FOR EXAMPLE, WHEN THEY TOOK STATISTICS CLASS.

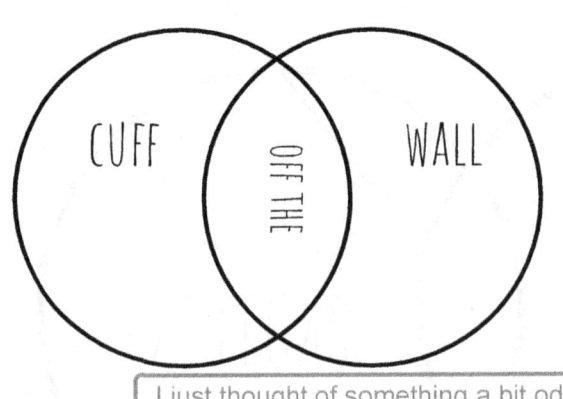

CUFF OFF THE WALL

I just thought of something a bit odd.

I **WONDER**... HOW YOU WOULD DO SOMETHING WITH, OR GIVE SOMETHING TO, SOMEBODY IF THEY WERE THE LAST PERSON ON EARTH, IF YOU AREN'T THERE ALSO?

SO...WOULDN'T IT BE THE LAST TWO PEOPLE ON EARTH?

I LIKE TO SAY,
"EVEN IF YOU WERE THE SECOND-TO-LAST PERSON ON EARTH,"
BECAUSE I'M AN OPTIMIST.

I LIKE TO THINK THAT THEY WOULD DIE BEFORE ME.

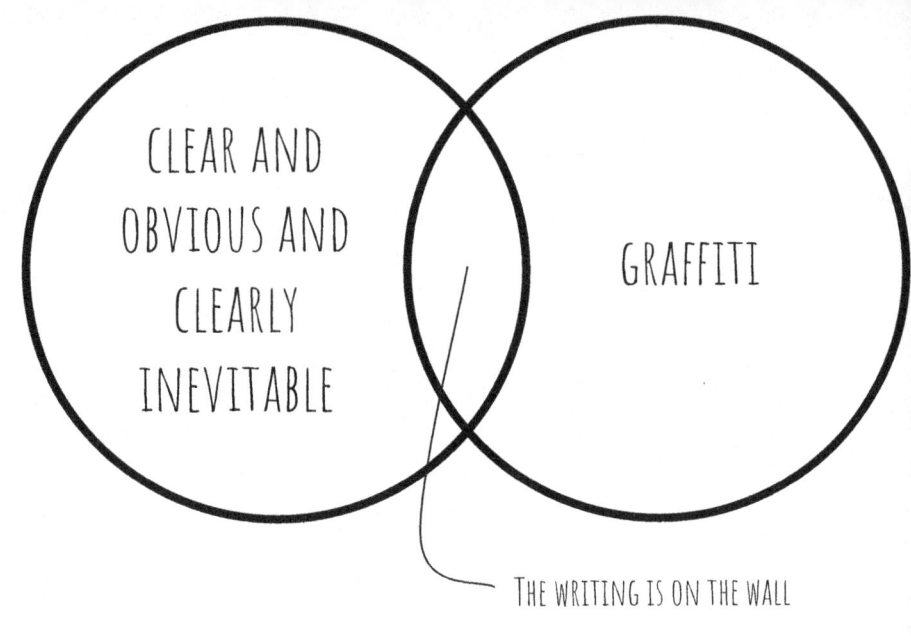

CLEAR AND OBVIOUS AND CLEARLY INEVITABLE

GRAFFITI

THE WRITING IS ON THE WALL

"HOMOPHONIES"

I'VE FOUND THAT *THYME* HEALS NO WOUNDS **AT ALL!**

I'VE ALSO FOUND THAT *HURTING CATS* IS ACTUALLY **NOT THAT DIFFICULT!**

AND I'M USUALLY **NOT BETTER OFF** IF I JUST GRIN AND *BARE* IT!

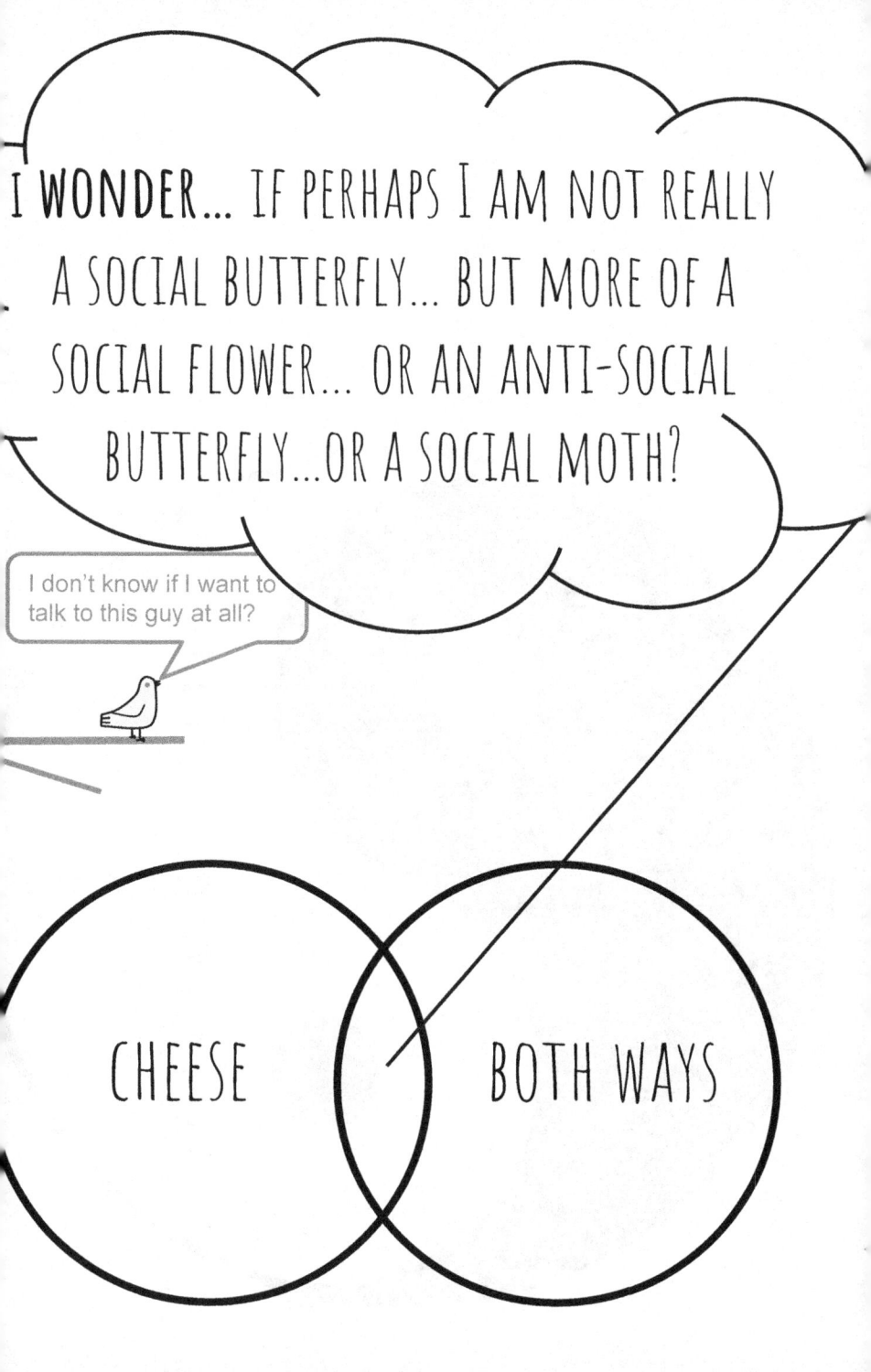

CUTS

ACTIONS SPEAK LOUDER THAN WORDS

THE PEN IS MIGHTIER THAN THE SWORD

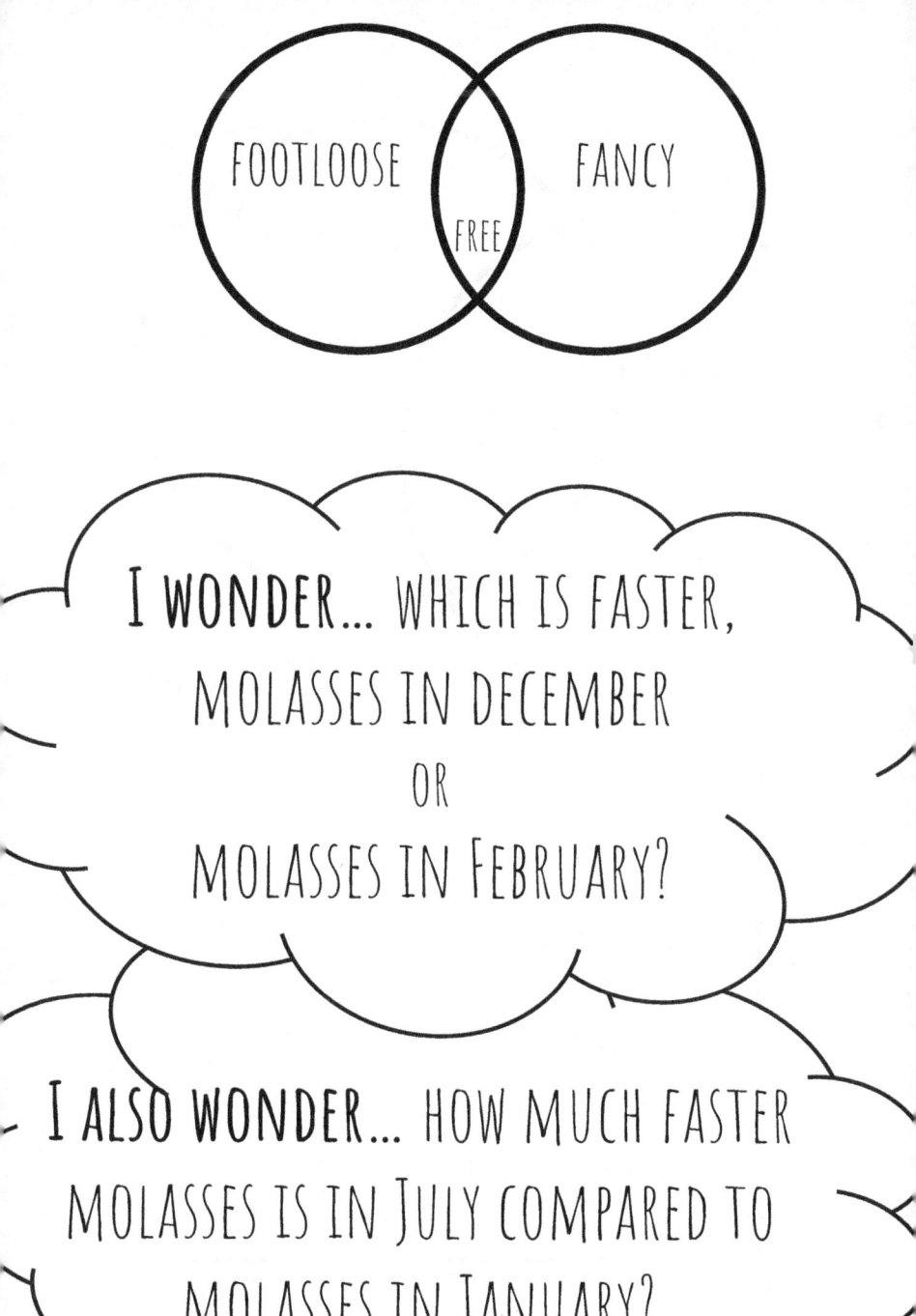

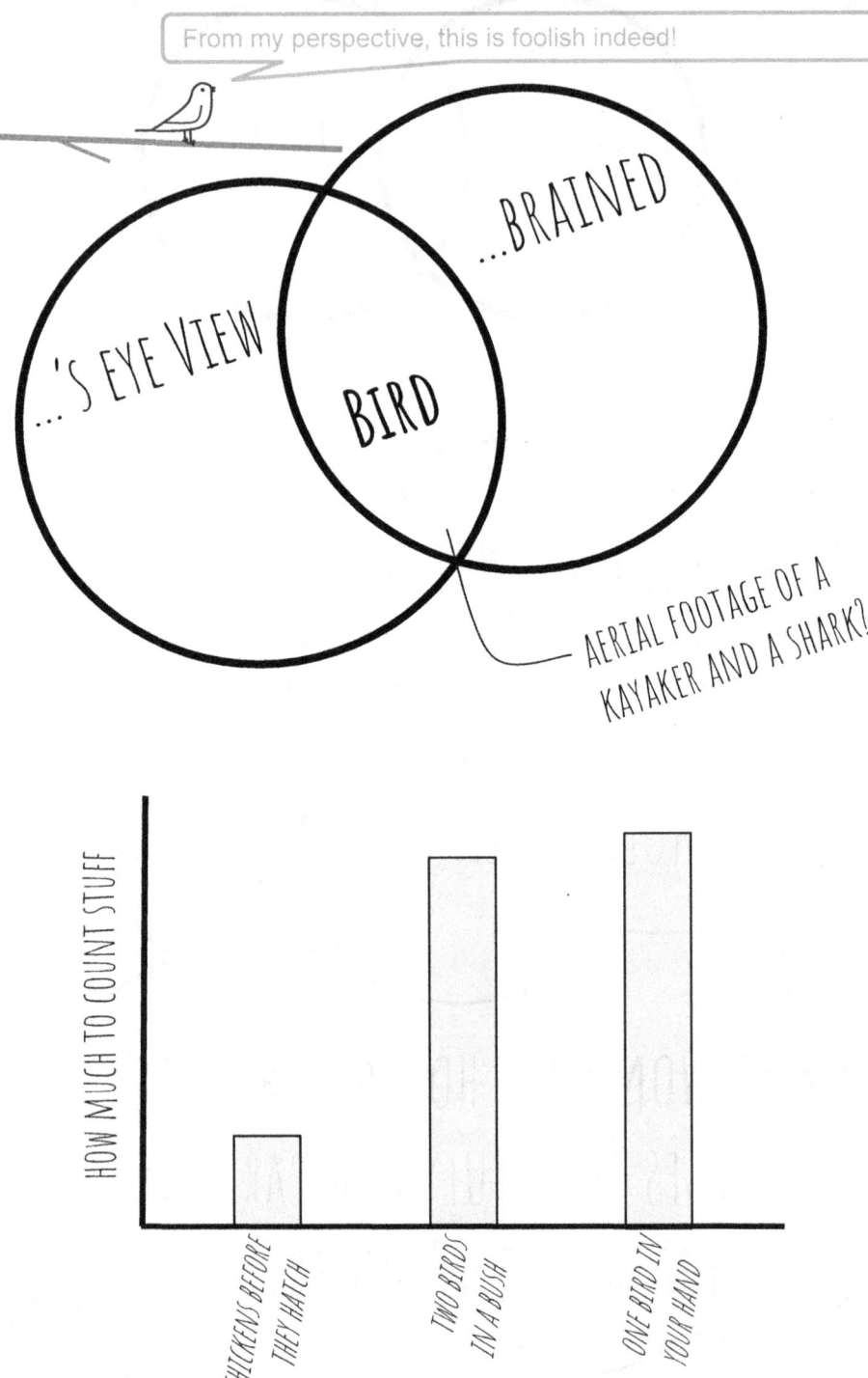

BUCDROPKET

YOUR FIRE BELLY

"I'VE DONE THIS SO MUCH THAT I'VE TOTALLY GOT IT."

BICORN

PEOPLE

CLOSENESS

STRANGERS ACQUAINTANCES FRIENDS ENEMIES

IF... AN OPTIMIST IS ½ DONE SHOVELING SNOW OFF OF A SIDEWALK, DO THEY SAY, "THIS SIDEWALK IS HALF EMPTY!"?

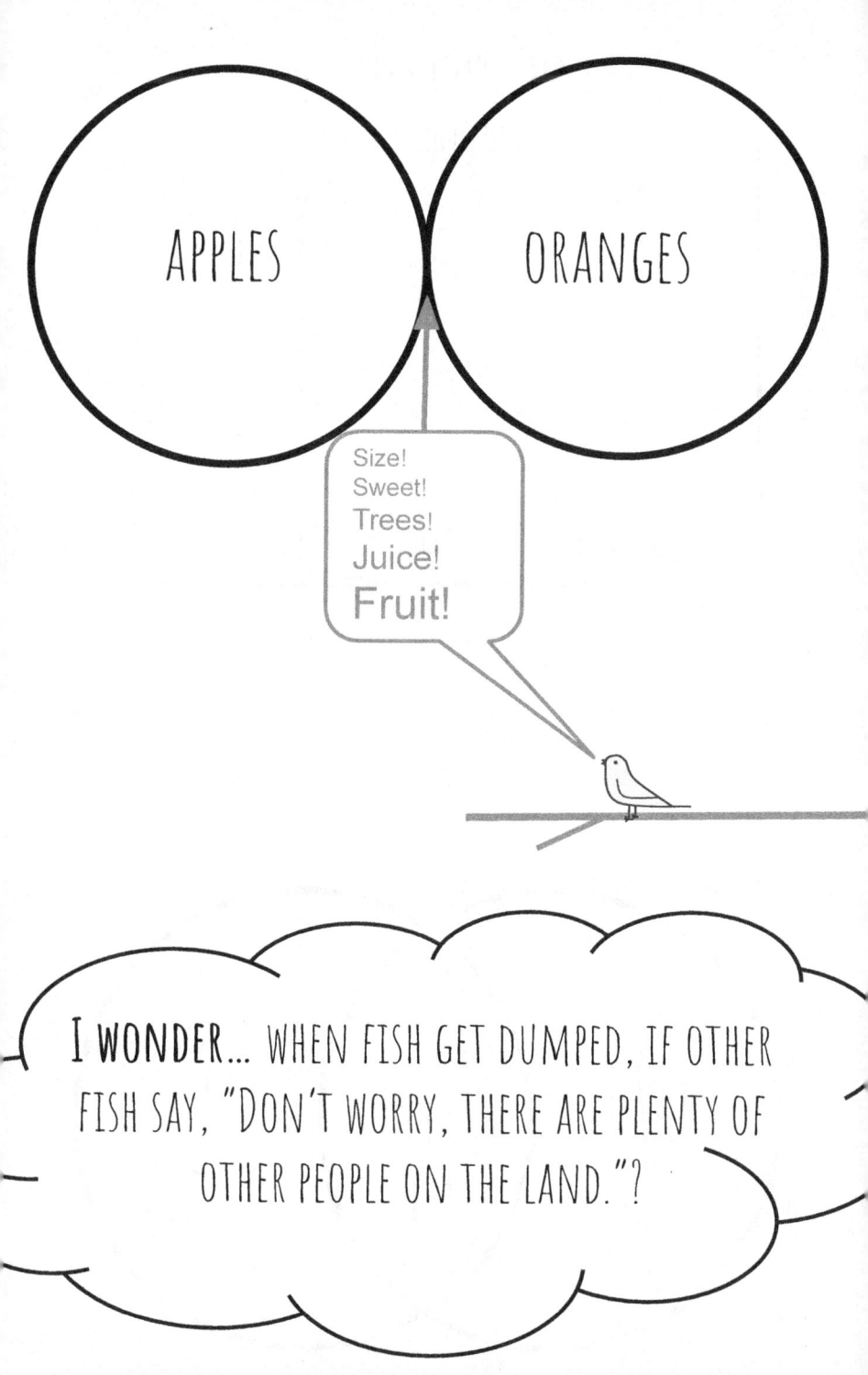

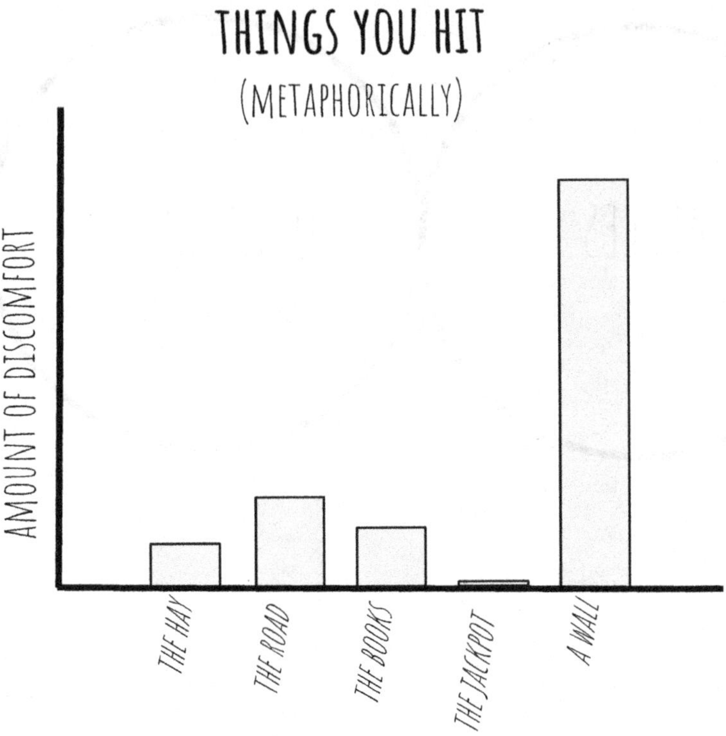
THINGS YOU HIT
(METAPHORICALLY)
AMOUNT OF DISCOMFORT
THE HAY
THE ROAD
THE BOOKS
THE JACKPOT
A WALL

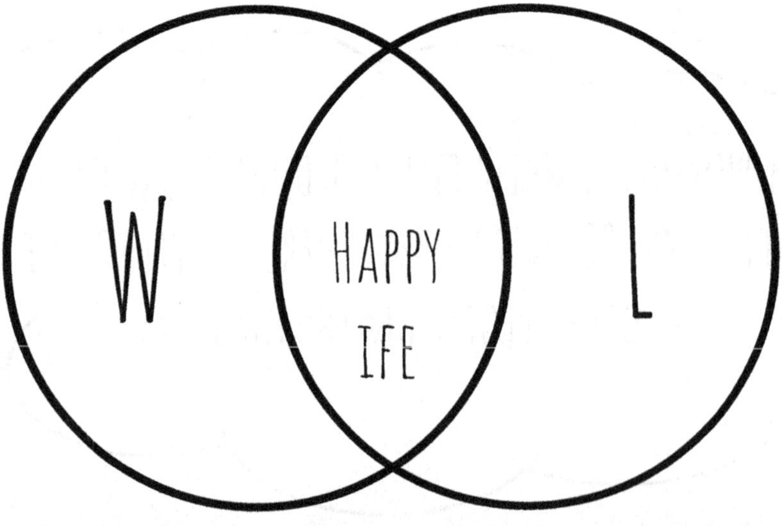
W
HAPPY
IFE
L

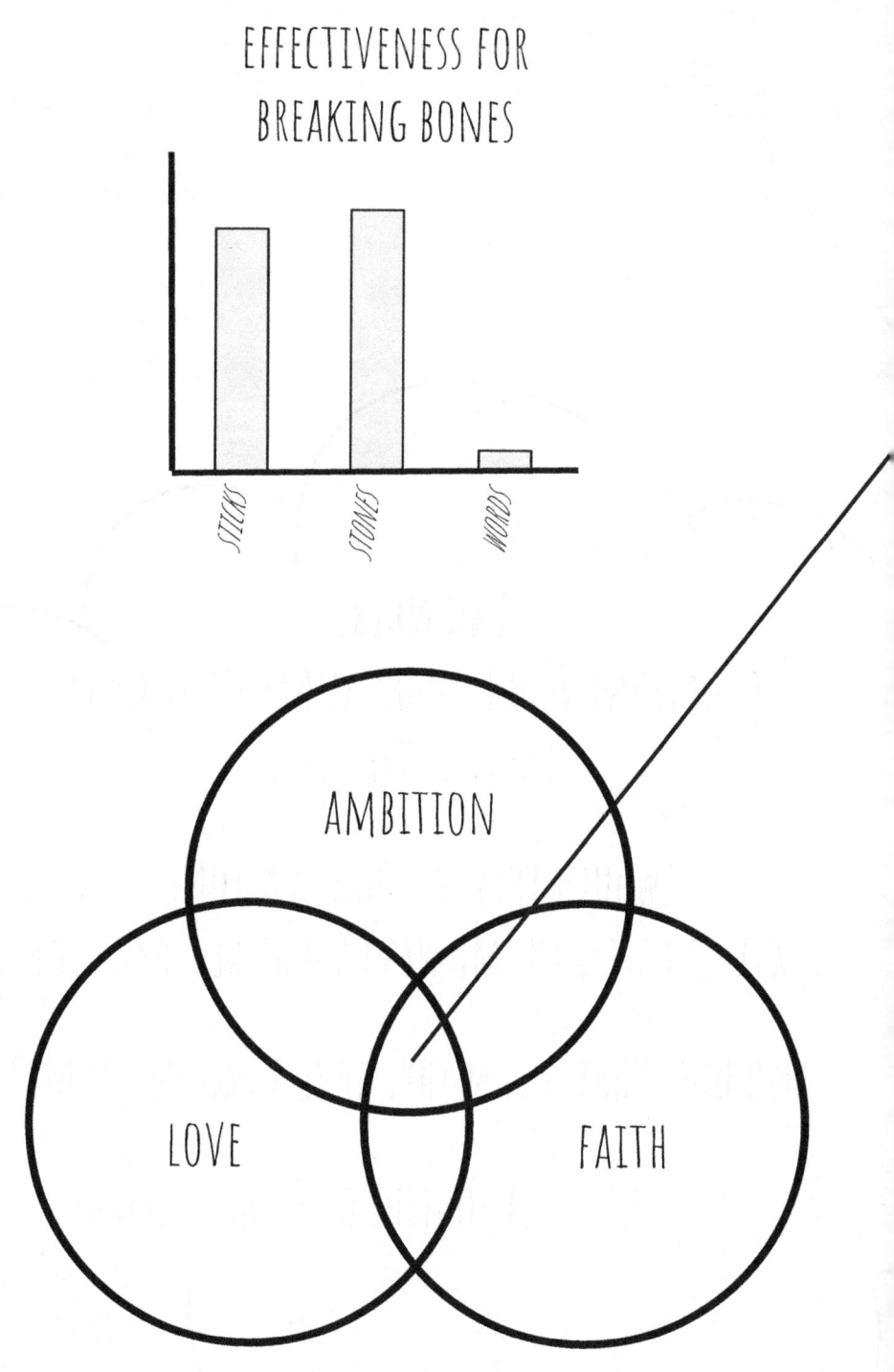

"A Day Late and a Dollar Short"
Idioms List

The orange that fell not too far from the tree

A forkful of sugar

The banana of my eye

A monkey's aunt

The people that gave 109%

The person that follows the silver rule

The light in the middle of the tunnel

Cat and pony shows

The unaddressed hippo in the room

The 700 pound gorilla

Alligator tears that get cried

When cows fly

The second-to-last straw

Cloud 8

Goody goody one-shoe

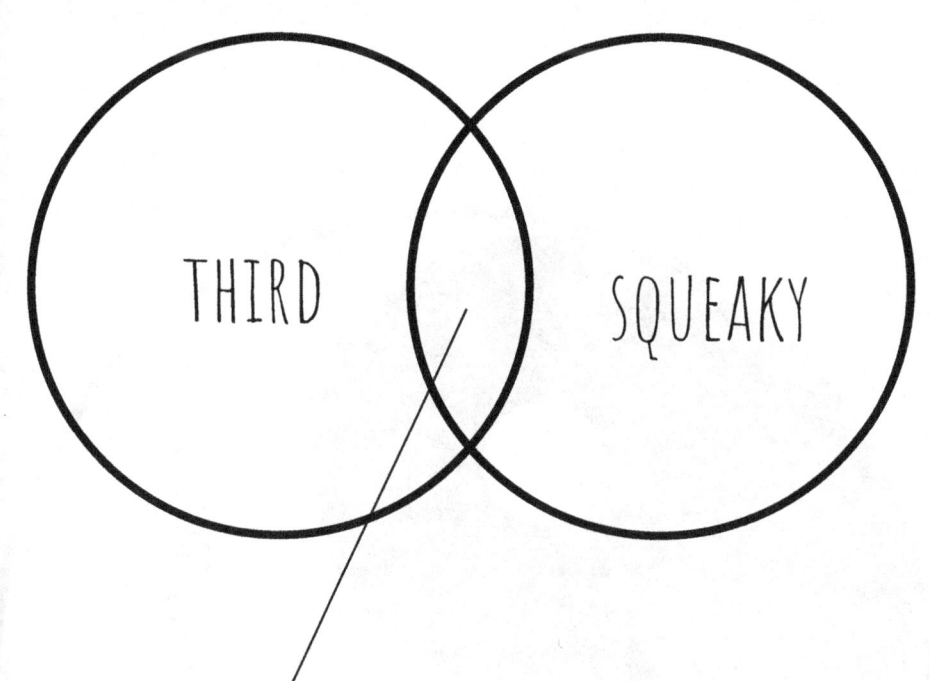

THIRD

SQUEAKY

I KEEP TRYING TO TELL MY WIFE THAT THE
DEFINITION OF INSANITY IS DOING THE SAME THING OVER AND
OVER AGAIN AND GETTING THE SAME RESULT.
NO MATTER HOW MANY TIMES I TRY TO EXPLAIN IT TO HER,
SHE JUST DOESN'T UNDERSTAND!

Put a lid on it, Buddy!

WHEEL

(NEITHER ONE IS WINNING A POPULARITY CONTEST)

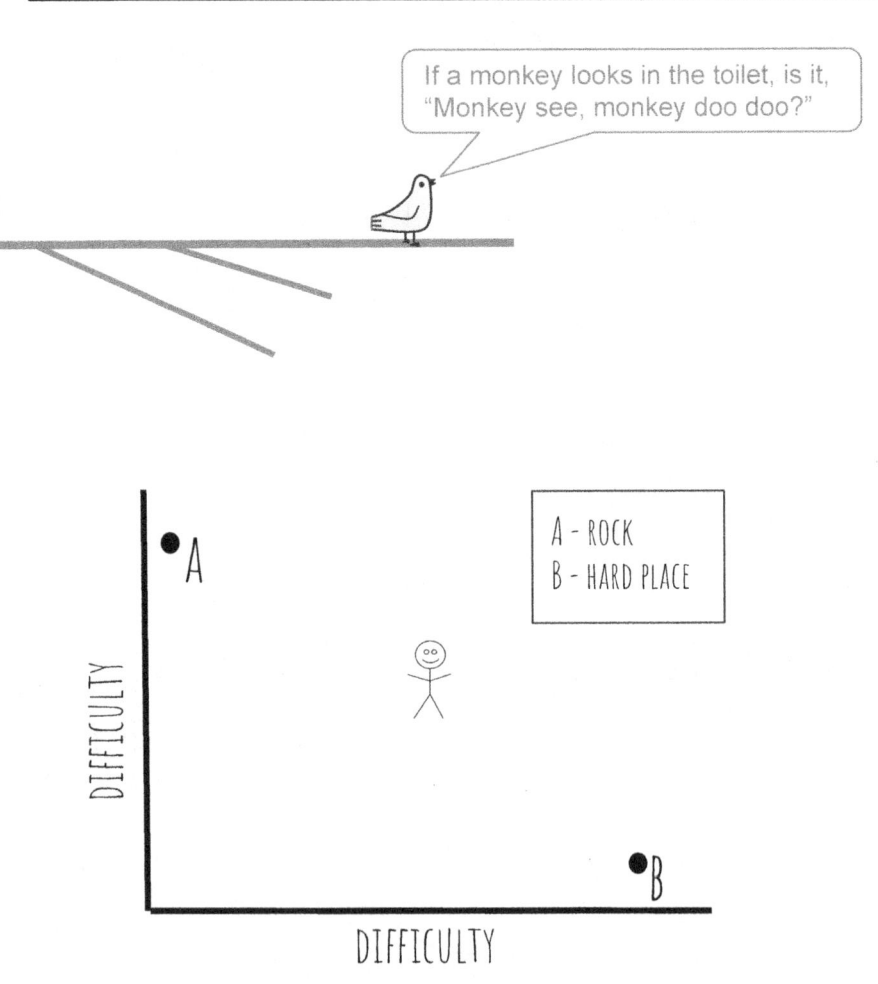

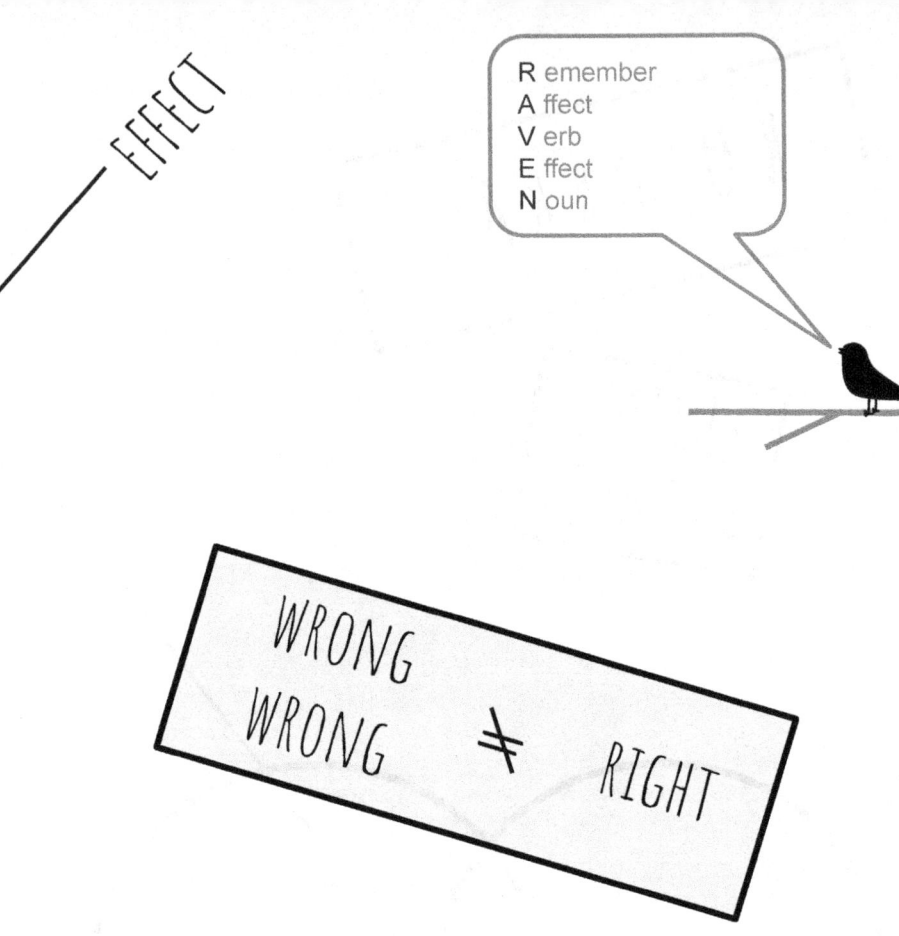

I THINK... THAT THE SOUND OF ONE HAND CLAPPING IS... SNAPPING

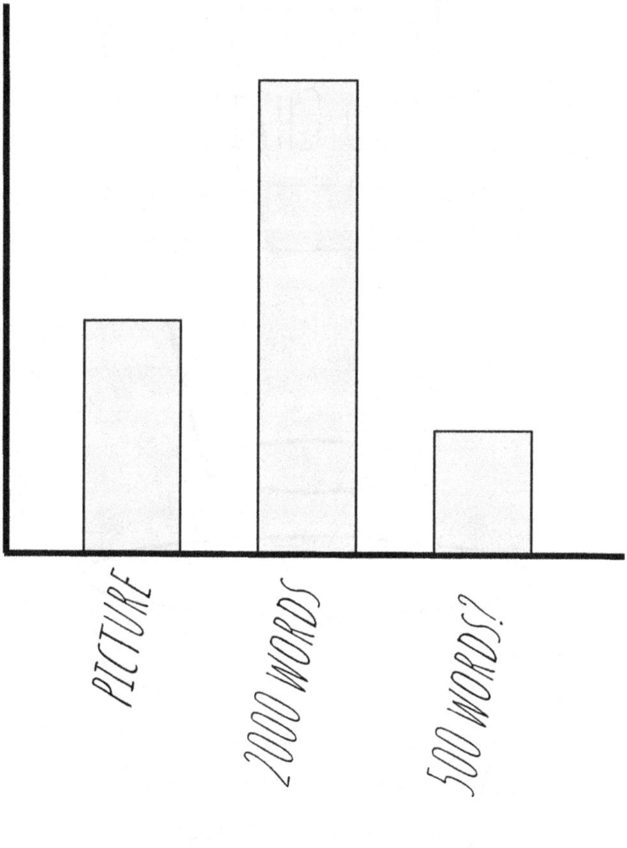
PICTURE
2000 WORDS
500 WORDS?

I wonder how many words Nolan Ryan is worth?

EVER WONDERED WHERE THE ROAD PAVED WITH BAD INTENTIONS LEADS TO?

BULLS   BIRD'S

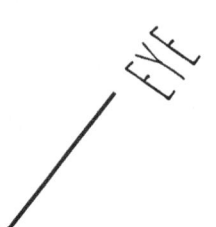
EYE

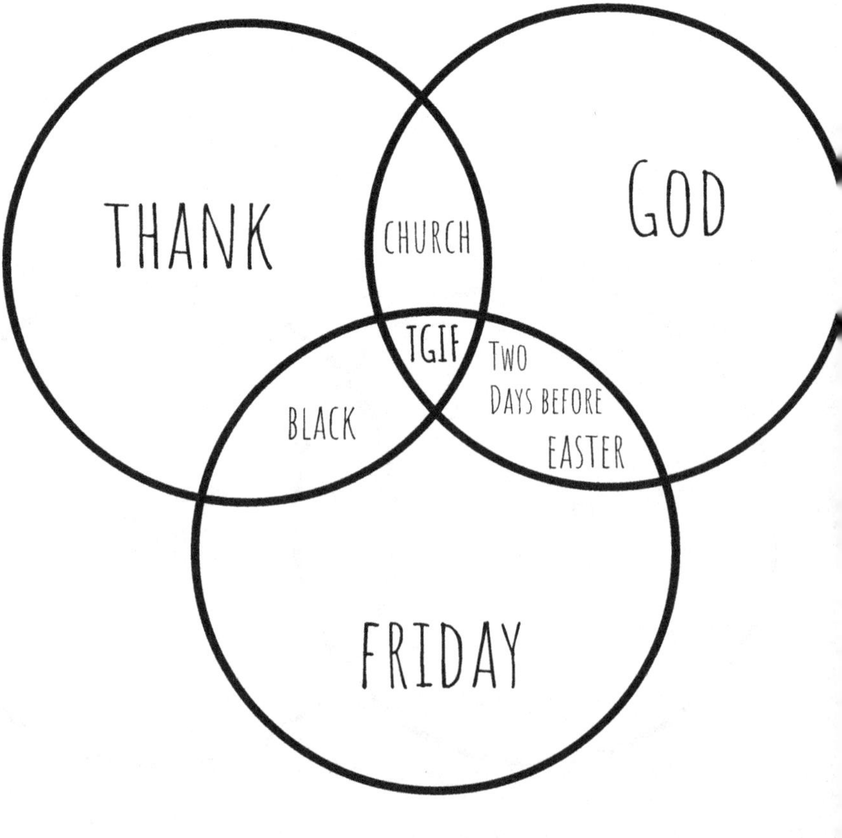

THANK

GOD

CHURCH

TGIF

Two
Days before
EASTER

BLACK

FRIDAY

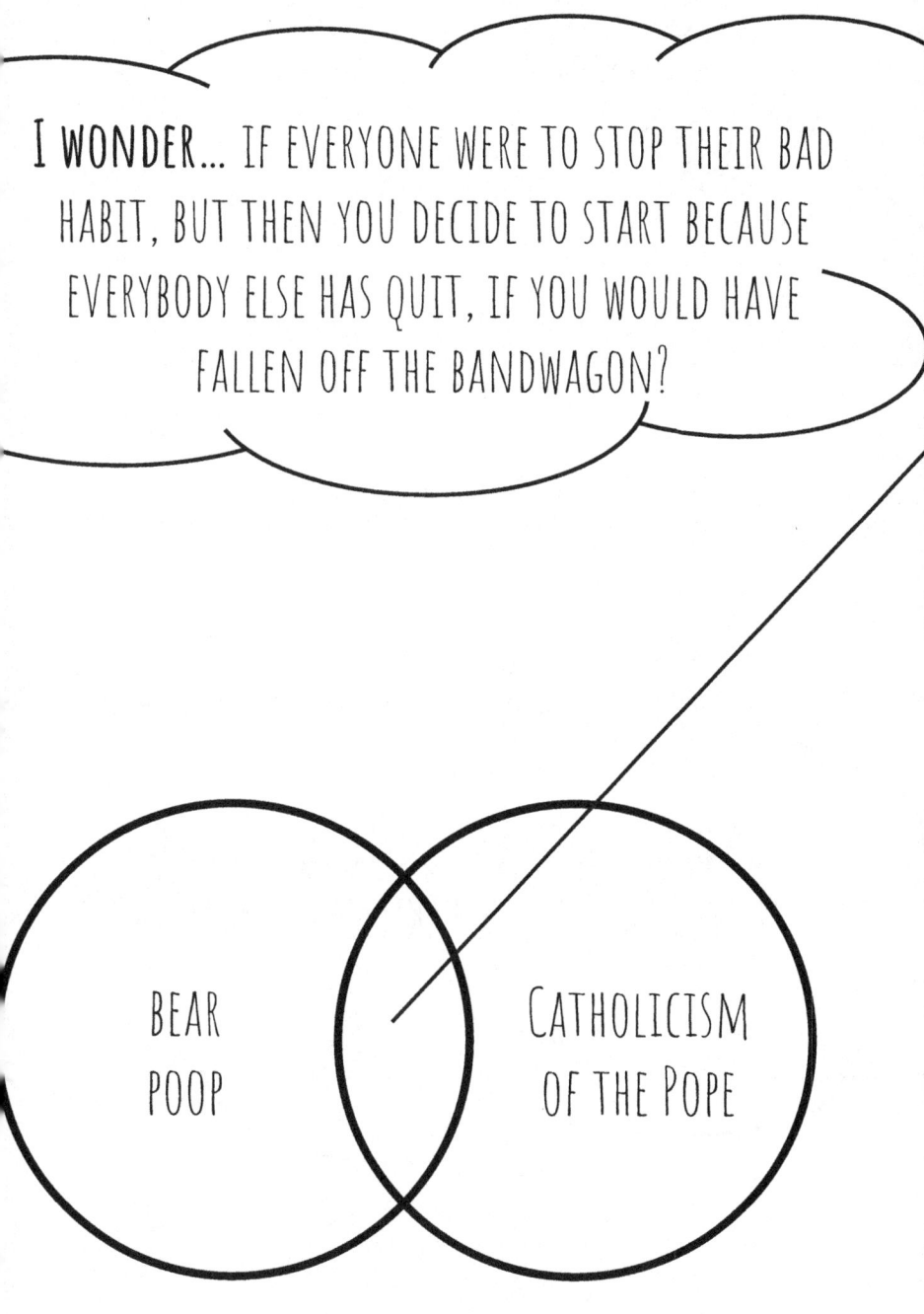

DUH!

I WONDER... WHEN CATS SLEEP FOR A LONG TIME, IF THEY'RE TAKING A HUMAN NAP?

I WONDER...
IF BUZZ ALDRIN WISHES UPON THE SECOND
STAR HE SEES AT NIGHT?

IF I WERE HE, I'D TWEAK THE IDIOM TO SAY,
A JOURNEY OF 1000 MILES STARTS WITH TWO STEPS?

IF I WOULD PROBABLY BE A BUFFALO BILLS FAN?

TO DO LIST

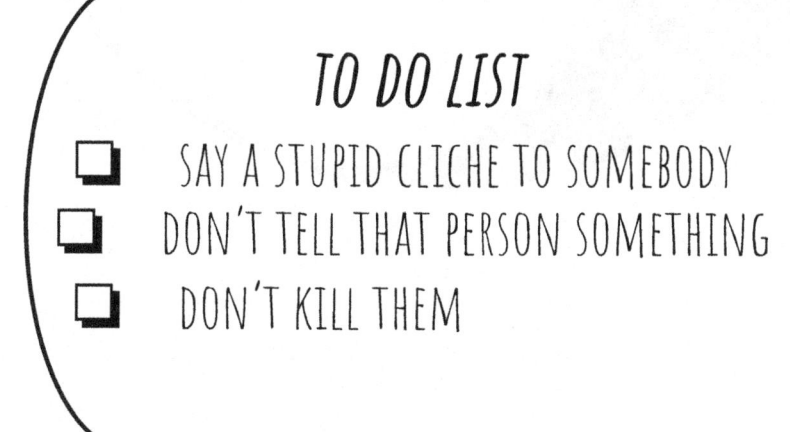

- ☐ SAY A STUPID CLICHE TO SOMEBODY
- ☐ DON'T TELL THAT PERSON SOMETHING
- ☐ DON'T KILL THEM

I TRY NOT TO DO ANYTHING BY THE SKIN OF MY TEETH. PRETTY MUCH BECAUSE MY TEETH DON'T HAVE ANY SKIN. MY GUMS? MAYBE. EITHER WAY, IT'S EITHER IMPOSSIBLE, OR GROSS.

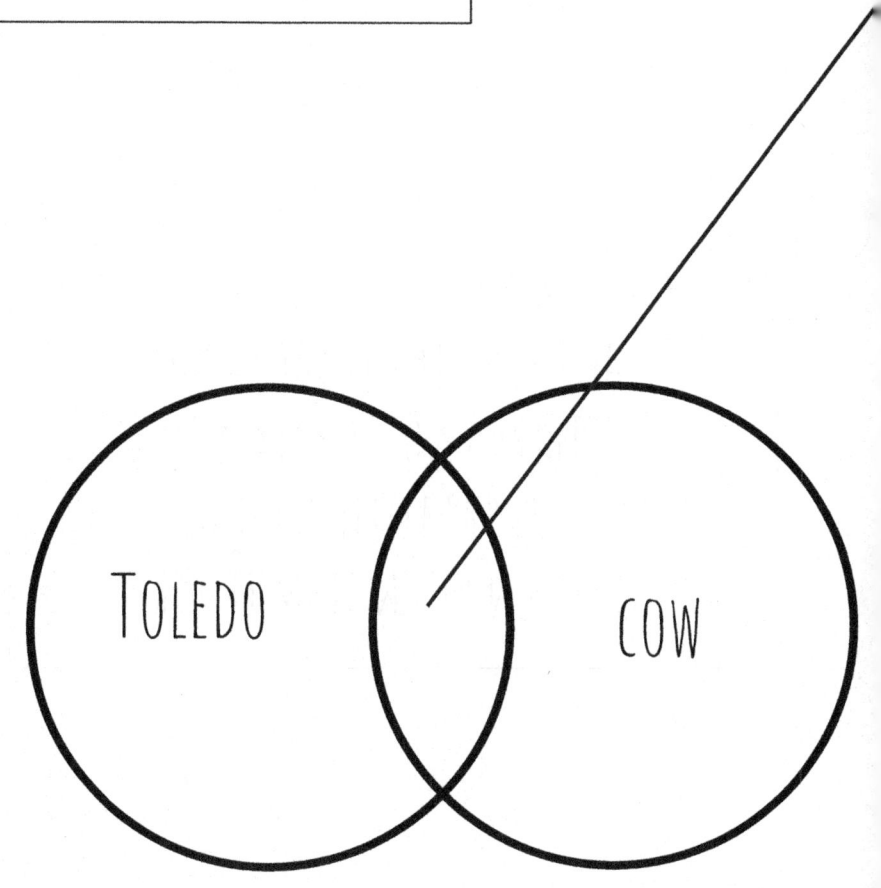

TOLEDO

COW

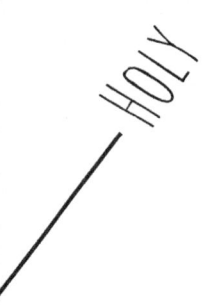

Moley?
Cannoli?
Guacamole?

> ANY TIME PEOPLE SAY TO ME,
> "THERE'S NO I IN TEAM,"
> I REPLY BY TELLING THEM,
> "THERE'S NO U IN TEAM EITHER."

There's an I in WIN!

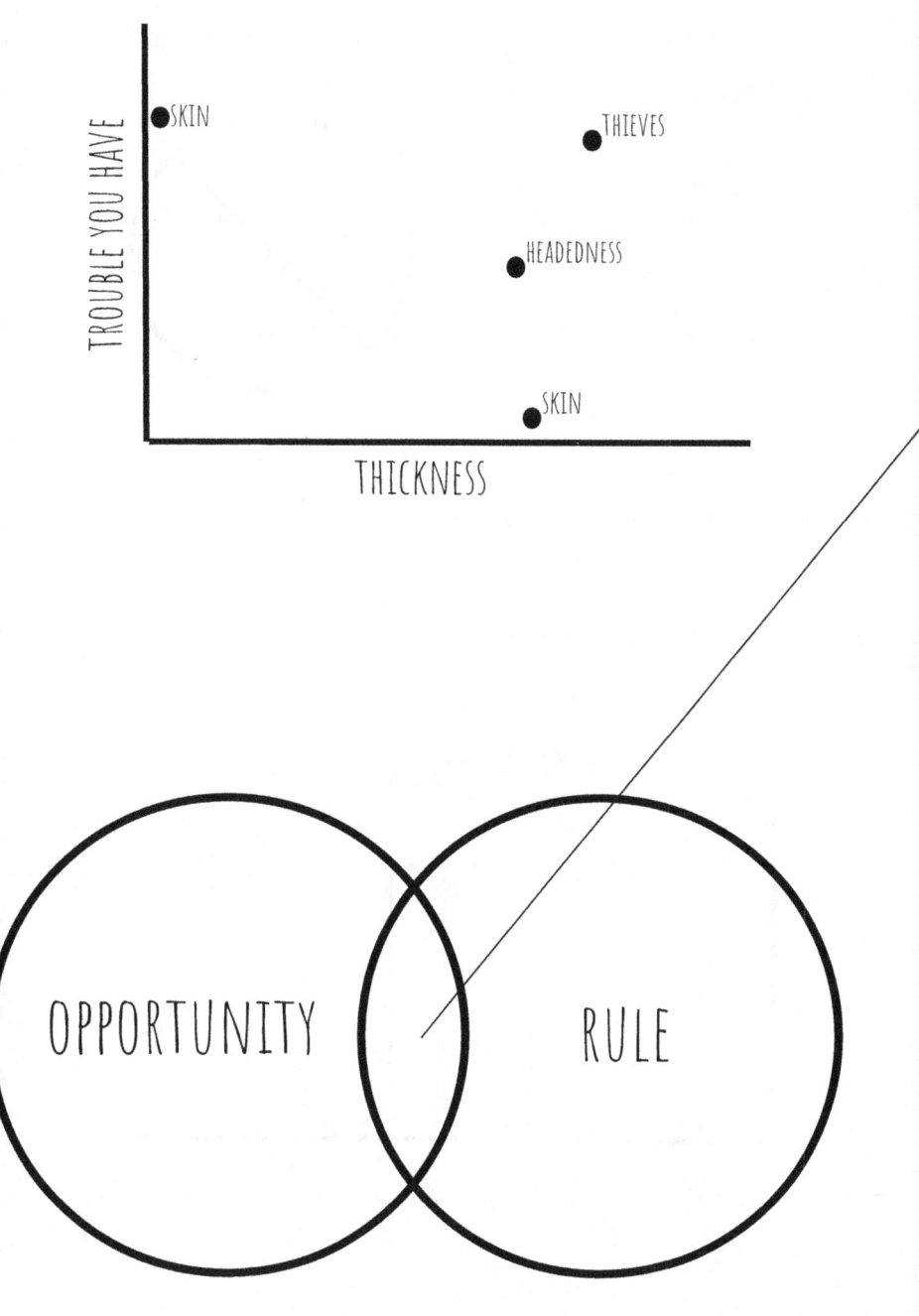

TROUBLE YOU HAVE

SKIN

THIEVES

HEADEDNESS

SKIN

THICKNESS

OPPORTUNITY

RULE

GOLDEN

THE WHOLE...

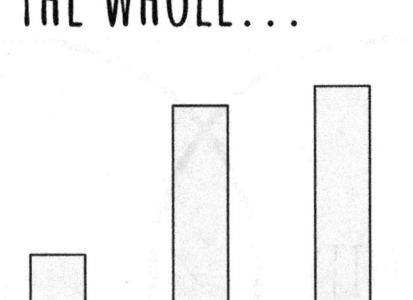

Not-English-ness

NINE YARDS · ENCHILADA · KIT AND KABOODLE · SHEBANG

JUSTIFIES

THE

MEANS

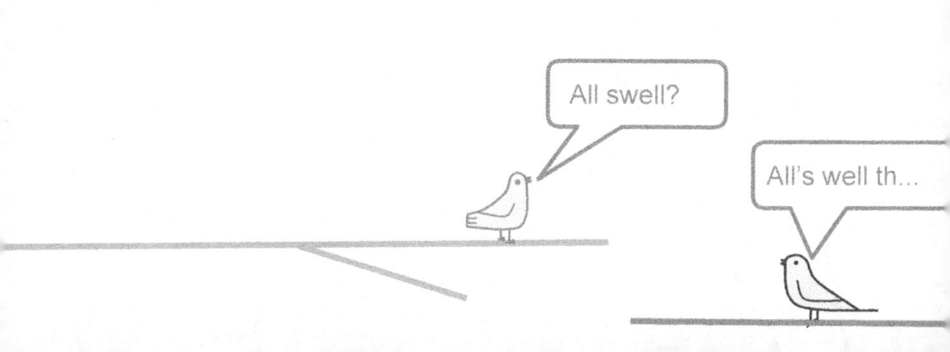

Made in the USA
Monee, IL
07 July 2026

56546295R00046